THE COMPLETE BEGINNER'S GUIDE TO
FISHING

The Complete
Beginner's Guide to
FISHING

GEORGE X. SAND

DOUBLEDAY & COMPANY, INC.
GARDEN CITY, NEW YORK

Contents

CONTENTS

LIST OF PHOTOGRAPHS

It is the author's sincere hope that the reader shall find this book friendly and easy to understand, and that it will offer atonement to those many still incomplete persons whose fathers, for some unfortunate reason best known only to themselves, could never find time to take their children fishing.

Foreword

No other human activity can offer the delightful combination of end-less expectation, sudden high excitement and sheer soul peace that fishing affords. No matter if one be young or old, rich or poor, in-telligent or backward, there is something about the simple act of wetting a line—even if only in a roadside ditch—that recharges the human battery in a manner defying description. Whether it be the body-restoring restfulness of some remote woodland lake, its silence broken perhaps only by the soft splash of a rising trout, or the happy shrieking of feeding gulls above a booming surf, there seems to be always present that certain potential for magic that is known only to the fisherman.

As someone once tried to explain it (with an angler's typical enthusiasm): "God does not deduct from a man's time on earth the hours he spends fishing."

What *is* that tugging you suddenly feel at the end of your line? Your pulse invariably races as you wonder whether you should take a chance and try to set the hook now . . . or wait just a moment longer . . . to make sure the investigating fish has the lure well in his mouth . . .

Then, back comes the rod, and—wow! Feel the solid weight of this fish! Look at him go! Surely this has *got* to be a fish of record size! (You know it very likely is not—but no matter.)

The excited angler may be but a barefoot farm boy catching a small catfish with a rusting hook and doughball bait. Or he may be a vacationing millionaire strapped in the fighting chair of a graceful Bimini yacht with a huge blue marlin leaping magnificently astern from the tropic sea. Yet the goddess of fishing luck will remain im-partial to both boy and man; she will invariably allow neither to be *sure* of landing his catch until the very last moment. And it is this very uncertainty that makes angling the fine sport it is—for all.

Why, then, it may well be asked, do not more people partake of the pleasures of fishing? The answer, I have come to believe after thirty years of firsthand observation, is that those so denying themselves fear that fishing is a sport that can be enjoyed only by experts. And, they tell themselves, they have neither the time nor money to become expert anglers.

I have written this book to show you that this is not true. In fact, if from what follows you learn but a *single* aspect of fishing—how to locate a fish's natural favorite food—you will have increased your chance of making a successful catch by at least 50 per cent. And, if you understand the remaining two basic considerations that determine the actions of nearly all fish—namely, what factors influence their comfort and safety—it should prove nearly impossible for you to miss.

I invite you to read on, and become convinced . . .

GEORGE X. SAND
Fort Myers, Florida

THE COMPLETE BEGINNER'S GUIDE TO
FISHING

Chapter 1
An Introduction to Fishing

The Hook

This least expensive item of your fishing equipment is also the most important. For it alone can determine the success or failure of even the most costly tackle. Without an effective hook at the far end of your line you may as well remain home. Unfortunately, many otherwise knowledgeable fishermen often make the mistake of using cheap hooks, even those completely unsuited for the task. An angler will exercise commendable care in selecting his rod, reel and line to provide a properly balanced outfit—then settle carelessly for any kind of hook, so long as it appears to be of suitable size.

Many fish are needlessly lost, as a result. Even worse, many of those that manage to rid themselves of the ineffective barb, and seem to escape, are often injured so badly in the process that they quickly become victims of sharks and other predators.

It is not known who fashioned the first fishhook. Probably it was done instinctively, just as small boys throughout the world today bend straight pins into "J" shapes, gleefully to snake small fish from the water.

Crude bone hooks have been excavated that were used by American Indians thousands of years ago. In those days a fishhook was nearly as important as a weapon, for both could be used to get food. Stones and other materials, even thorns, were also used by early anglers. Later, when metals came into use, Roman citizens fashioned fishhooks from bronze. Some of these have been identified as early as A.D. 79. And before Columbus discovered America, natives of the Amazon made hooks of solid gold, since that precious metal was plentiful at the time.

To be effective, however, a fishhook must have the strength that best comes from correctly tempered steel wire. The metal must not be too brittle, else the hook will snap apart under pressure. Conversely, if the metal is too "soft," the hook will bend uselessly. (Unfortunately, both these undesirable characteristics can still be found in certain cheaply made hooks today.)

Until the fifteenth century fishing hooks had to be individually made. Then the English began to mass produce hooks, using tempered steel wire. Soon they were supplying anglers throughout the world, and many of their early barb designs are still in use. Since then, however, the United States has also become a world leader in this field.

One American manufacturer, for instance—the Wright & McGill Company—the leading producer of fishhooks in this country—uses high-speed, automatic machines to turn out more than two million of their Eagle Claw barbs every day.

Wire used in producing fishhooks is first handled in the annealed state in the factory. (That is, after it has been subject to heating and slow cooling, to toughen the steel and reduce brittleness.) After machine fabrication, the hooks produced from such wire are heat treated and tempered again, in atmospherically controlled furnaces. The barbs are then cleaned, colored or plated, then packaged for shipment and customer use.

The cheapest hooks made today are simply given a blued finish. This is not a durable coating, and soon permits the steel underneath to rust. The hooks least subject to rusting have no finish, but are made of stainless steel, instead. Some barbs carry a bronze finish. Others are plated with nickel, cadmium—even gold—to hinder rusting. Once a hook's protective finish is scratched, however, it becomes subject to rusting. The finish may be broken from fish bites, from snagging against submerged objects, and—quite commonly—from honing or filing the barb, something every good fisherman does to keep his hooks sharp and effective.

A shiny new cheap hook will, unfortunately, often appear to be quite as sturdy as a good hook. There are various snagging, and pulling power, tests that one can make. But it is seldom convenient to do this at the time of purchase. If you have reason to question the advice of the seller, make inquiries at fishing piers, boat docks, etc. beforehand—particularly, seek advice from guides and commercial fishermen. They will be able to recommend good hooks.

A hook is manufactured by bending back upon itself a piece of steel wire into one of a variety of shapes, each of which has been found best suited for a particular fishing need. These shapes will vary from so-called worm hooks, which are designed best to hold a real or plastic worm in position, to tuna hooks. There are barbs best suited for dressing a fly, and others specially bent so a jig can be designed upon the shank. Snelled hooks come with a short leader already attached. Other barbs may be of weedless design, with a small wire guard extending from tip to bend, to prevent snagging. (*Figure 1–1*

Figure 1–1 First drape rubber band over shank of hook, then pull free end back through eye, as shown. Next, stretch band to barb, and secure there.

shows how you can use a rubber band to make a hook weedless, in similar fashion.)

Some barbs have special grippers on the shank better to hold natural bait in position, and prevent it from bunching up at the bend, thereby possibly preventing the barb from finding lodging in the fish's mouth when the strike comes. Other hooks are designed to accommodate a single salmon egg, and so on. *Figure 1–2* illustrates some of the most popular Eagle Claw hook shapes. Note that hooks are made not only in single barb design, but also, double—and even treble (a cluster of three barbs on one shank; the last hook is used mainly on plugs and other artificial lures, although it also works well—when manufactured with a small brass spring over the shank—to hold dough, cheese, blood and other soft baits.)

Some hooks are made with the eye in the same plane as the shank. Others have eyes that bend upward or downward from the shank. Shanks, in turn, may be long, short or have special bends. It is easier to "sew" (secure) a long-shanked hook inside a balao, and certain other natural trolling baits (as is explained in Chapter 3) than it would be to do this with a hook of short shank. On the other hand, the shorter hook would work better for making a fly, as discussed in Chapter 4.

Sometimes it is advantageous to bend a long-shanked barb to form a "keel" hook, as shown in *Figure 1–3*. With its center of gravity

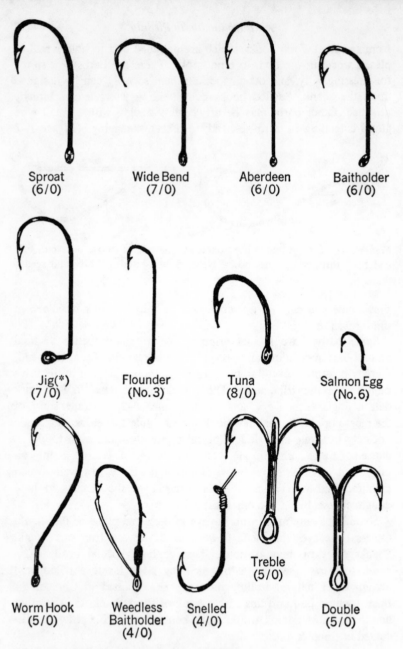

Sproat (6/0)   Wide Bend (7/0)   Aberdeen (6/0)   Baitholder (6/0)

Jig(*) (7/0)   Flounder (No. 3)   Tuna (8/0)   Salmon Egg (No. 6)

Worm Hook (5/0)   Weedless Baitholder (4/0)   Snelled (4/0)   Treble (5/0)   Double (5/0)

(*For manufacturing lead-head jigs.)

Figure 1–2

Figure 1–3   Keel Hook

thus lowered, the keel hook moves through the water with the point up. Hence it is less apt to catch upon grass and other bottom obstructions. Keel hooks may be purchased, too.

The numbering system used to designate hook size (refer to *Figure 1–4*) may confuse the new angler. For some reason, the numbers

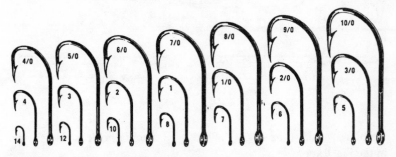

Figure 1–4   The hooks shown are the most popular sizes, others range from the tiny No. 22 ($\frac{3}{32}$ inch) to the huge meat hooks used when fishing for sharks. (Courtesy of Wright & McGill Co.)

decrease in value at the outset to indicate an *increase* in hook size. Then, when the zero—or reference—point on the scale is reached, the system reverses itself. The numbers now increase to indicate an increase in hook size. And, to confuse the beginner further, some hooks are designated by seemingly inappropriate names like Sproat and Aberdeen and O'Shaughnessy. In time, however, such things will become clear to the newcomer.

As shown in *Figure 1–5*, the extent of a hook's "bend" determines the size, or "bite." To make it possible to tie the hook securely to the fishing line (or leader) a small ring, or "eye," is formed in the "shank" at the opposite end from the bend. It is the "tip" portion of the bite that first pierces the fish's mouth when the strike is made. And the "point" portion of the hook includes a "barb" that helps keep the tip embedded. Should the bend of the hook be manufactured in such a manner that it is not in the same plane as the shank, then

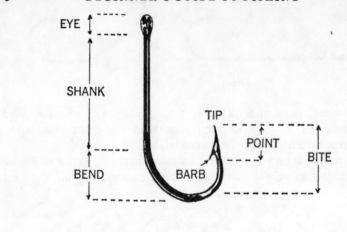

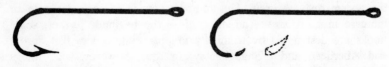

Figure 1–5

the hook is said to be of the "offset" type. Such a hook is also shown in the illustration.

I have some angler friends—especially those who consistently seek record catches—who prefer to "triangulate" their hooks before use, to provide better penetration. To do this, the point and barb are carefully filed to provide three separate cutting surfaces, as shown in *Figure 1–6,* instead of the customary single point.

Figure 1–6

The Leader

A better name for the "leader" might be "follower," or even "joiner," since this short additional section of the line (usually only a foot, or two, when used—although fly line leaders may be six feet, or more) invariably follows the hook. It joins the hook to the main portion of the line, as shown in *Figure 1–7.*

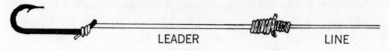

LEADER   LINE

Figure 1–7

Since the presence of a leader demands at least one additional knot—and the presence of *any* knot makes your line weaker than it was before—a leader should be used only if there is a need for it. The tapered leader performs a special function for the fly fisherman, for example, as will be discussed later. Too, a monofilament leader, because it is less visible to fish than a conventional line of Dacron, or some other material, can produce more strikes under certain conditions. Again, the added protection provided by a shock leader (one purposely of greater breaking strength than the line) can serve you well when fishing for species with sharp teeth (mackerel, for example), or fish that may have rough skins (the shark is one) or abrasive mouths (like snook and tarpon) that can quickly cut through, or fray apart, a lighter line. Too, oyster bars, barnacle-grown pier pilings and similar submerged obstructions have sharp edges that will cut through a line not protected with a heavier section at the end.

Monofilament is used most for leaders today. A foot or two of 20 to 30 pound breaking test mono is usually sufficient to protect the customary 8 to 15 pound test fishing line. For large game fish—sailfish and tarpon, for instance—50 to 100 pound mono leaders, sometimes wire, are used for trolling and casting. Wire may be either solid (piano wire) or braided. Wire is stronger, and is available in strengths of 300 pounds, or more. But it adds weight to a terminal rig—sometimes enough weight to jeopardize the "action" of some light tackle artificial lures when these are cast out and retrieved. Too, unless a dull-finish wire leader is used for some species, the fish may strike at the flash of the wire, instead of the lure. And wire has a bad habit of kinking and breaking during a hard struggle with a fish, particularly, solid wire.

The Swivel

A swivel is usually positioned between line and leader. Its main purpose is to reduce line twist, brought about by turning motion of the terminal equipment during casting, retrieving and trolling. The swivel also serves as a handy means of knotting together two lines—

particularly, a line and a wire leader. And a swivel with a snap that can be quickly opened and closed at one end serves as a convenient way for changing lures, when it is used at the end of the line or leader, closest to the lure. (Certain snap swivels are more dependable than others, however, so let your choice be guided accordingly.)

Swivels come in different sizes and shapes, as shown in *Figure 1–8*. Note how numbers are used to designate sizes of the popular

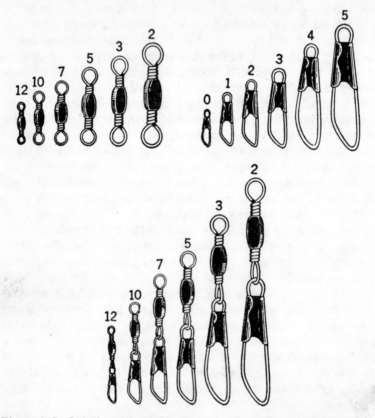

Figure 1–8 Swivels (upper left), Snaps (upper right) and Snap-Swivels (Courtesy of Weber Tackle Co.)

"barrel" (or series) swivels, and that these numbers *decrease* with increase in swivel size. The three-way swivel is popular with bottom fishermen and surf casters. It tends to hold separated from one another the line, leader and sinker—thereby reducing risk of tangling.

The Sinker

Lead is the material used most commonly for sinkers. It is heated to the molten state, then poured into molds corresponding to the various sizes and shapes preferred by fishermen. (Some of the most popular of these are shown in *Figure 1–9*.) Anglers who frequently

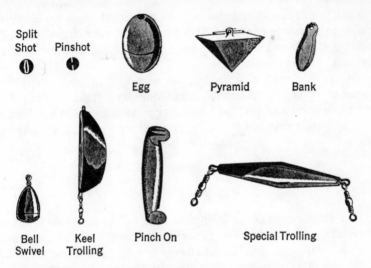

Figure 1–9   (Courtesy of Royal, Division of Norton Mfg. Co.)

lose sinkers find it a saving to buy such molds and make their own line weights.

Some sinkers, like the pyramid type, are designed to bury quickly into a soft bottom. There they hold the bait securely in position, hopefully, to await the arrival of foraging fish. Surfmen use the pyramid weight to a large extent.

Conversely, when it is intended that a bait should not remain in one spot, a so-called "egg" sinker may be used. This rounded weight has a hole through its center that permits a fishing line to pass back and forth, unhindered, when the sinker is purposely not tied fast. Hence, when fishing with such a terminal rig, it is possible for a bait to be washed freely back and forth by bottom currents. Such movement can catch the eye of some fish that might otherwise remain unaware of the bait's presence. It also allows a live bait to swim freely. And should a wary fish pick up the bait its suspicion will not be aroused by the unaccustomed weight—something which can cause certain species of fish to drop the offering immediately.

Another kind of sinker, the so-called "keel" type, moves through the water in an upright position at the end of a trolled line, resisting the tendency to spin, as an ordinary weight might do. This discourages unwanted line twists and general fouling. A second type of trolling sinker that is used to get a bait or artificial lure down to where the fish are, is one that has no keel but depends upon other means to prevent line twisting. This other sinker, often pencil-thin and pointed at each end, depends upon "bead chain" swivels, each with a snap, at both extremities.

One of the simplest of weights, and very easy to use, is the elongated crimp-on, or "clincher," type. Some light tackle anglers, flycasters in particular, prefer a small circular variation of this sinker: a tiny split-shot that can be easily crimped into position on line or leader.

The Line

The development of the fishing line, like that of the hook, seems to have taken place gradually. History is vague concerning how lines slowly evolved through use of stringy lengths of tree bark, animal hair and other thin substances, twisted together to provide added strength—much as natural and artificial fiber lines are still made today. There will be readers of this book who, like the author, can recall the days when a good fishing line was not only quite expensive but annoying to use. That is, such a line required careful drying after each use, to prevent rotting. Too, it required waterproofing and other time-consuming care. Those of us who could not afford a good silk or linen line had to settle for cotton—or, sometimes as a last resort, waxed shoemaker's thread!

By the end of World War II, there emerged from American chemical laboratories several exciting new fishing lines: extruded monofilament and braided lines of Dacron and nylon. Widespread use of these new lines was aided considerably by the appearance of a new style of fishing about this time, also: spinning. Since then, it appears to many that mono has become the most popular of the new lines. Everywhere one goes one sees anglers using monofilament. Nevertheless, the Cortland Line Company—the world's largest manufacturer of lines—points out that fishermen still spend as much money on braided lines as they do on the monofilaments.

The initial cost of a braided line is higher, and understandably so. For additional processing steps are required in the factory. The lines must be doubled, twisted, heat-stretched, dyed and waterproofed—in addition to the usual careful breakage testing—before the product is finished. But in time the braided line often proves to be the best investment. For it has a longer life than monofilament.

Too, a braided line has a notable lack of stretch, which means the angler has a better chance of setting the hook. And this line will usually prove easier to handle on the reel, particularly a spinning reel. It does not form into springy, bothersome loops the way monofilament is apt to do. And it often spreads more evenly on the spool of a level-wind type reel. Too, a braided line generally permits the angler to "horse" a stubborn fish better; also, more often to pull loose valuable lures that have become snagged on some obstruction, either below or above the surface. The majority of world record fish catches have been made with braided linen, Dacron or nylon lines.

For many years fly lines were made of braided silk. These lines were heavily impregnated with oils to give them the weight necessary for proper casting. Too, the user of a floating type fly line in those bygone days had to keep it dutifully lubricated. If not, it would sink. Often the flycaster might have to pause in midstream to "grease" his line! Then, happy day, there appeared on the market fly lines made with a snake-belly-smooth plastic coating which no longer required lubricating. These new lines could be picked up from the water—and cast—with an ease hitherto unknown. Some of the lines employed tiny air bubbles, trapped in position inside the fly line body as a function of the manufacturing process. This made the line non-sinkable.

Hardly a year passes that improvements do not continue to be made in fishing lines. As this is being written, for example, Cortland has just announced its Micro-Foam fly line, which, the company proudly explains, "features a small Micron core surrounded by countless gas-filled air chambers for highest flotability."

Imagine . . . casting a gas-filled line!

The Rod

Fishing rods fall mainly into four types, as shown in *Photo 1:*

bait casting, spinning, fly casting and heavy duty (for trolling and big game fishing). There are, in addition, some multi-purpose—and other special—rods made. For example, some companies manufacture what they call a "spin-cast" rod that is suitable for both spinning and bait casting.

The term "bait casting rod" can be confusing. Such rods were used originally to cast bait, both live and dead. Today they are also popular for casting jigs, spoons, spinners and plugs—especially the last. All these artificial lures are also habitually cast with spinning rods.

Before we discuss further the various kinds of rods, let's consider how they are made. Elderly fishermen will recall the days when nearly every rod was made of split bamboo, or other cane. A good one was quite expensive; the others were prone to warp ("set") easily. All were fragile.

An attempt was made to substitute various metals for the bamboo. But these whippy rods left much to be desired; too, they were prone to corrode and rust. Then "glass" rods appeared. These sticks, made of glass fibers in resin, could not rust. And the casting ability of a carefully designed fiber glass rod could be made to approach closely that of the best cane rod.

There are two main approaches in the making of such a rod. Some manufacturers prefer to start the construction process with glass cloth that has been tightly woven, both vertically and horizontally, from thousands of tiny glass fibers. Others feel that a stronger rod can be made simply by running the threads parallel to one another, the full length of the rod.

In the first case, a template is used as a guide to cut a piece of glass cloth of the size and shape that experience has shown will be needed to manufacture the specific rod being built. The cloth has been previously impregnated with a plastic-based liquid resin, then allowed to dry partially, so that now it is in a tacky state. This will permit the cloth to be rolled evenly, and under great pressure, about a round steel rod, or mandrel. This blank is then subjected to changing temperatures, inside a curing oven, after which the mandrel is removed and the rod is polished and trimmed. Finally, the line guides and other hardware items are installed.

The longitudinal fibers of the second style of fiber glass rod are likewise impregnated with a plastic-based liquid resin for bonding. Here, instead of the amount of cloth used, it is the number (thickness) of the fibers used that will determine the rod's diameter, its action (stiffness) and so on. One manufacturer, Shakespeare, uses a reinforcing cylindrical wall of glass fiber inside, with thousands of parallel glass fibers outside this. This company feels that when glass cloth is used the fibers may work against each other and break.

In selecting a rod for purchase the beginning angler will invariably encounter the phrase "balanced tackle." A balanced fishing outfit is simply one that has been selected to provide maximum comfort and efficiency for a specific user. That is, the rod, reel, line and lure are matched to one another to provide greatest casting comfort, accuracy and so on. The beginner would find it difficult, for example—if not impossible—to cast effectively a light lure with a heavy rod. Similarly, if one attempted to mount a heavy, trolling type, reel on a light casting rod, it would so unbalance the rod that the would-be user would quickly become hopelessly tired. The need for balanced tackle is of special importance in fly fishing, where the line—not the lure—provides the necessary casting weight, as we shall see in Chapter 11.

Bait casting and spinning rods generally fall into one of these classes of lure-handling ability: ultra-light, light, medium and heavy. An ultra-light bait casting rod would be used to cast lures of about ¼ ounce, whereas a spinning rod in this especially light category could cast effectively even lighter lures, as small as ⅛ ounce. A medium bait rod would handle a ⅝-ounce lure, with the equivalent spin stick performing best with a slightly smaller lure, perhaps one of ¼ ounce. Heavy rods in each case could be expected to handle lures of ¾ and ½ ounce, and up, respectively.

The lure-handling ability of a rod should not be confused with the rod's action. The action of a rod is determined by its ability to "load" (i.e., bend backward from the vertical, during casting preparation, to shoot the lure forward), by the speed with which the tip returns to the stationary position, and other characteristics that will be discussed in greater detail in following chapters.

Bait casting rods usually measure between 5 and 6 feet in length; spinning rods, from 6 to 7 feet. A spinning rod intended for heavy use, however (usually in salt water) will measure from 7 to 11 feet, with some surf casting sticks even longer.

Fly rods come most often in lengths between about 7½ and 9 feet (special rods may be somewhat shorter, or longer) and may vary in weight from about 3 to 6 ounces. The longer the rod, the easier it will be to pick up line from the water. The heavier the rod, too, the better your chance of casting the line properly in windy weather, in open areas. Such a big rod can call for a strong arm, however. For the beginner, an 8- or 8½-foot length is usually best. More on such matters later.

Caution: Cheap fishing tackle, much of it foreign-made, continues to flood the American market. I know of no certain way to distinguish between a good and a poor rod before use. The poor one can be made to look equally attractive and dependable. I can only suggest that you purchase from one of the long-established manufacturers; or, at least, from a reliable store.

The Reel

We have spoken of bait casting, spinning, fly casting and heavy-duty rods (the last for trolling, and big game fishing). Matching reels are available for use with each of these rods.

The bait casting reel (*Photo 2*) consists of a handle-rotated line spool that is positioned between two round, sometimes elongated, end plates. These plates are separated by pillars (spacers) and each plate serves as an end bearing for the spool. Inside one end plate, the thicker of the two, there are gears that cause the spool to revolve as many as five times for each full turn of the handle (although 3:1 and 4:1 ratios are most common). The spool revolves first in one direction as line is pulled out (either by the weight of a cast or trolled lure, or by a fish), then in the opposite direction as line is retrieved by turning the reel handle with a forward motion.

Kentucky watchmakers are credited with building the first of these "revolving" reels, back about 1800. The basic principle of operation has changed little since then, although several refinements have been made. One of these is the level-winding mechanism. Whereas once the angler was obliged to use the fingers of his free hand to position the returning line evenly across the spool surface—this to avoid the uneven build-ups that reduce casting efficiency, and cause backlashes—today a slotted mechanical finger does this instead, with gear-driven precision.

Another improvement is built-in anti-backlash control. When a bait or lure is cast out there is a tendency for the rapidly revolving spool to overrun from its own momentum: that is, to turn at a rate faster than the speed of the departing line. This can cause a backlash, or "bird's nest" as some disgusted fishermen call it, for that is what the tangle can resemble. There was a time when only precise thumb pressure applied against the spinning reel spool—something learned only after much practice—could prevent this annoyance. Today, however, good revolving reels come equipped with a built-in means for applying friction to the spool to prevent overrunning. (An automatic centrifugal brake is one means for accomplishing this.) The amount of spool friction is controlled by an external adjustment on the reel.

Still another refinement is the free-spool feature. When a lever on the reel is operated the spool is disengaged from the gear chain (although the level-winding mechanism may continue to operate) and the spool is free to revolve substantially unhindered. This not only makes for longer, easier casting, it also spares the angler's knuckles from contact with rapidly whirling reel handles—something that can prove painful when a large fish is tearing off line!

When purchasing a bait casting reel make sure that the spool starts easily and operates quietly—then stops quickly when even a small amount of braking is applied. A spool made of aluminum or other light metal is preferred to one that is heavy, and therefore may continue to revolve longer when the reel handles are given a spin. For the added momentum of the heavier spool can invite overrunning and subsequent backlash.

There should be an absolute minimum of clearance between the spool and the end plates. If not, the small-diameter monofilament lines in use today are apt to enter these openings and disable the reel action. The reel should also be well constructed, of course, and should be made of rust-resisting metals.

A spinning reel, by contrast, see *Photo 3,* cannot backlash, since the spool remains stationary when a cast is made. The reel's open-faced spool points in the same direction as the rod (instead of crossways to the plane of the rod, as did the revolving, or bait casting, reel just discussed). This permits the outrunning line to leap from the fixed spool in spirals, or coils. These are straightened out as they pass through the line guide on the rod.

When line is to be retrieved—following a cast, or after a fish strikes—the reel handle need be turned in a forward direction only for a short distance to activate the reel's rotating head, or spool cup. Meanwhile, a mechanical line catcher (i.e., either a full or a part bale) flips into position before this cup to engage the line and start winding it back upon the spool—one layer of line being deposited thus for each turn of the reel handle.

(This bail pickup is pushed back with the free hand, and locked in position out of the way, each time before a cast is made.)

Some anglers prefer to remove the bail from a spinning reel permanently, leaving only the associated line collector guide. They then use the forefinger of the rod-holding hand (the finger next to the thumb) to pick up the line upon retrieving. This can be done, with some practice, by catching the cast-out line on this finger, then lifting it into the retrieve position upon the line collector that is mounted on the outside edge of the revolving spool cup. Some line collectors consist of a moving roller; other guides at this position are merely made of shallow-grooved, extra-hard metal to resist wear from the passing line.

The spool of a spinning reel turns only when line is being pulled out—as by a struggling fish—and this turning is prevented, to the extent that the angler wishes, by an adjustable drag. The drag is actually a friction clutch—one that can be set to start slipping, to let the spool start to turn, just before the breaking strength of the line is reached. In some cases this breaking mechanism is contained inside the removable spool.

A second style of spinning reel—sometimes called a spin-cast reel, since it can also be used on a bait casting (even a fly) rod—is not open-faced. Instead, the spool and line pickup and release mechanisms are mounted either completely, or at least partly, inside an enclosed housing, or hood, as shown in *Photo 4*. With this reel the line moves in and out through a small hole in the center of the housing, or nose cone. The drag adjustment is located outside the housing, for easy accessibility, and a control trigger—perhaps a button—is also mounted externally for control of the outgoing line during casting. When line is retrieved this reel operates in a manner similar to the revolving, or bait casting reel.

Both styles of spinning reels eliminate backlashes that one is apt to encounter while using a revolving reel. However, tangles can result while spinning: for example, should a loop slip from the stationary spool out of sequence, as sometimes happens when the returning line has not been deposited evenly. (The oscillating type action that causes the spool to move in and out of its protective cup during reel winding, thereby laying down loops that cross one another, instead of lying parallel to one another, seems to be the better of the two systems for avoiding this type of tangle.)

Spinning reels, the open-faced type particularly, have the annoying tendency to form twists in a line—particularly when used to fight a strong fish, or while trolling.

It is easier to cast with a spinning reel—which makes it ideal for beginning fishermen—and one can cast farther with it than he can with a bait casting reel. The revolving reel provides greater casting accuracy, however. And most anglers find that it enables them to handle large fish better. On the other hand, the spinning outfit handles small lures better. And it often seems more sensitive to the fish's action.

In purchasing a spinning reel make sure that the spool is easily replaceable, and offers sufficient line capacity for the kind of fishing you intend. The reel should give evidence of sturdy construction, and should have a good finish, to resist wear and corrosion. Put some line on the spool, tie the end to a sturdy support, then—with the drag on—walk backward to test the smoothness, and the strength, of the drag at various settings. A jerky, uneven drag is a promise of even more erratic behavior later.

Unscrew the cover of the gear housing and inspect the mechanism within. A good spinning reel employs a ball bearing anchor gear train. There should be an anti-reverse control, externally operated and mounted on the reel within easy reach, to prevent the reel handle from flying backward, should the handle slip from your grasp while battling a strong fish. If there is too much clearance between the spool and the frame (i.e., the spool cup), line is apt to slip into this opening and wind about the drive shaft. The reel should be capable of easy lubricating, even while in use, and it should come apart easily for overhaul and cleaning, after use.

Bait casting reels may vary in line capacity from perhaps 150 yards of 10 pounds test, to 600 yards of 20 pound. Spinning reels range from about this same lower limit to maybe 400 yards of No. 20 as the maximum. Ultra-light spin reels may accommodate 200 and 300 yards of No. 2 and No. 4 line, respectively. Gear ratios will vary from about 3:1 to 5:1.

A fly reel, however, is usually direct drive—1:1 ratio—whether it be of the handle-operated or automatic type (see *Photo 5*). This means that there are no gears involved. The spool revolves once for each turn of the reel handle, or, in the case of the automatic reel, it turns directly as line is pulled out.

The automatic reel has no handle. The outgoing line loads a spring; the more line that is pulled out, the tighter the spring is wound.

Then, with the touch of a finger from the rod hand, this spring operates to retrieve the line. Usually, an overrun, or slip, clutch prevents a strong fish from injuring the spring after it has become fully wound. These little reels are not suitable for handling large fish.

An automatic fly reel will accommodate about fifty yards of 20 pound backing line, in addition to the thirty-yard (average) fly line. The average single-action reel will accommodate a maximum of about 150 yards of backing. In recent years heavier styles of single-action fly reels have been developed (see again *Photo 5*). These reels incorporate powerful built-in drags and are used for large salmon, billfish, tarpon and other big gamesters. Some cost in excess of a hundred dollars each. These reels, which will be discussed in more detail in Chapter 11, can hold 250 yards, or more, of backing line.

With the exception of the powerful fly reels just spoken of, the fly reel serves mainly as a means for storing the line, and, to a lesser extent, to balance the weight of the rod, to make casting easier.

A single-action fly reel is built somewhat like a bait casting reel, save that it is considerably larger in diameter and the spool is quite narrow (both these design features permit quick retrieving of the fly line, when necessary). An axle extends from the center of the rear, or tail, plate and the spool slides into position over this axle, after which the spool is secured in place with a threaded spool cap. The handle is attached to one edge of the outer spool face. The material used for the single-action fly reel is very light metal, usually aluminum, and simplicity is the keynote in design and operation of this reel.

Trolling and big game fishing reels are simply heavier—and, in the last case, much more expensive—versions of the bait casting reel already discussed. These reels are shown in *Photo 6* and will be described in greater detail in later chapters.

Other Tackle

While it is true that only a rod, reel, line and baited hook or artificial lure are needed to go fishing, there are certain additional items of tackle that can make the sport more enjoyable by the angler. For instance, a landing net or gaff—depending upon the size of the catch you expect to handle—will insure that the struggling fish does not escape when it is ready for boating or beaching.

By "ready" I mean that the fish should be completely exhausted. A catch that is still "green"—a large fish, especially—can not only injure an angler, but break his rod, too. Chapters 10 and 11 explain how to net and gaff fish properly.

Nets come with the frame (called the "bow") shaped in various styles to meet different needs. A D-shaped bow, being straight at its front edge, is best suited for dipping bait, or scooping along a bottom, for example. Other nets may have round, or pear-shaped bows. Net bags are woven of cotton, nylon, plastic and other material, and may vary in depth from one to three feet, or more. Net handles, like the frames, are usually made of aluminum and vary in length from about six inches to six feet. Some are adjustable (telescopic). The shortest handles are usually on belt nets.

Gaffs may have metal or wooden handles. They vary in size from small belt gaffs to heavy, harpoonlike affairs. These last are called "flying gaffs" since they can be hurled at a fish, with retrieving rope attached. (Some anglers question the sportsmanship involved with this style of gaffing, since it would indicate that the fish has not been completely—and fairly—subdued by the angler.) The bite, or size, of the (usually) barbless gaff hook will depend upon the size of fish to be handled.

Chapter 7 discusses waders, boots, wading shoes and other items of apparel required by the wading angler.

A sturdy fiber or metal rod case is almost a must for the angler who does much traveling to fish. Such containers are usually round, with a removable cap at one end. The larger ones may accommodate as many as six rods of medium bait casting and spinning size. Some of the cases are adjustable, to fit rods of varying lengths. The best case I've found for my own need—since most of the trips that I make call for but two average-size rods, three at most—is a hinged aluminum rod case (made by Garcia). It is 3 inches wide by 1¾ inches deep and is available in lengths of 40, 45 and 55 inches. Foam cushions inside this sturdy, easily handled case protect the rods—two of which are easily carried; three, if you wish to crowd.   •

Tackle boxes are nearly always made of plastic or aluminum. This is done to avoid rust problems, and to keep the carrying weight as low as possible. (For some such boxes provide as many as 124 lure compartments, and such tackle, along with reels, etc., can be heavy.)

Tackle boxes come in a variety of sizes and shapes. (Some of these designs are shown in *Photo 7*). A box may be of the single tray type, hence substantially flat. Or it may have a hiproof, to permit a half dozen, or more, hinged trays to spring upward, and outward, when the box is opened. One box resembles an attaché case, and will hold a traveler's (six-piece) type fishing rod, in addition to providing space for lures, reels, etc. Another tackle box has pull-out, individually lidded plastic lure boxes instead of trays. It also serves as a seat for the owner.

Some fishermen prefer to carry their tackle in shoulder or belt bags of leather or cloth.

Most tackle boxes appear to be best suited for the fresh water angler. The saltwater man often finds that many of the trays are too small for the hefty plugs and other large lures that he uses. Too, his reels are often bigger, and require more bottom space in the box.

The secret is to select a tackle box best suited to your specific need. Perhaps two boxes would serve you better: one for boat fishing, the other for shore use; or one for fresh water, the other for salt. The wading angler, of course, is limited to the use of lure wallets or small plastic fly and bug boxes that he can stuff into the pockets of his vest or jacket.

The shore fisherman, notably the surf caster, will find it advantageous to use a rod butt holder that straps about his waist and which makes it easier to hold his long stick while standing and waiting for a strike. Too, a sand spike will come in handy to hold the rod while he is rebaiting, or changing tackle.

The big game fisherman likely will wear a special chest and waist harness to prevent a big fish from pulling him bodily from his fighting chair. But, like the chair, this equipment is usually provided by the boat owner, and remains on board.

Bait buckets, nets and traps will be discussed in Chapter 3.

A hook disgorger, pliers for shaping and cutting leader wire, and similar tools are also important items of the angler's tackle. So is the fingernail trimmer that many flymen use for trimming the ends of leader knots. There are also gadgets for tying knots, for threading leaders through the tiny eyes of small flies and so on. The beginner will gradually accumulate such things after observing other anglers using them, and after recognizing the need for such aids.

Chapter 2
Fishing Knots

The knot is one of man's earliest inventions. Yet from the beginning—from the time he discovered how to make a vine doubly useful by tying its end to that of another—man has associated the knot with fumbling confusion, mystery—even fear and power.

It was once believed by superstitious ancients that if a rope were knotted about the body of a sick person, then removed and fastened about a tree, or some other object, the illness could be transferred, leaving the person cured. Or a sorcerer might make a well person ill simply by repeating the intended victim's name while tying a certain kind of magical knot.

In the era of Christ, the historian Pliny recorded the square knot as being used by Roman soldiers to tie bandages on the battlefield. And those master knot tiers, the Egyptians, apparently feared to reveal their methods. For, while the remainder of their historical tomb drawings might reveal amazing detail, the knot design was invariably obscured.

The early Orientals used knotted cords to symbolize power, and to send coded messages. The Peruvian Indians tied knots to take a census, record taxes or make a calendar. Later, sailing ship sailors depended upon properly tied knots not only to keep straining canvas aloft, but also to log water depths and time and speed. (Hence the expression "knot" for a nautical mile.) The American Indian knotted his tepee together with leather thongs. And the cowboy carefully fashioned a running noose in his lariat.

History reveals, in fact, that over three *thousand* kinds of knots have been developed. Some of the best fishing knots in use today came into existence shortly after World War II, when monofilament line appeared on the market. This new plastic line, known as nylon at that time, proved too slippery to use with the familiar knots that had worked well until that time with cotton, linen and silk lines.

Make a waterfront survey today and you will discover that perhaps not one fisherman out of any hundred knows how to tie even half the sixty-odd knots being used by salt and fresh water anglers. Many fishermen continue to use inadequate knots that slip, pull apart and even cut into the line under strain. They do this because no one has taught them how to tie proper knots, or because they are reluctant to learn.

Much controversy exists over what constitutes a good fishing knot. I have expert angler friends who will argue hotly whether a surgeon's knot or a blood knot is best for joining monofilament sections of different diameter. Admittedly, some of the best knots can prove exasperating to tie at times—while seated in a rocking ocean skiff, for example, or perhaps standing in midstream, fly fishing: the nail knot, for instance (although I shall shortly explain a new, and easier, way to tie this one). But it is a matter of either tie the proper knot or risk losing a choice fish.

If the beginning fisherman—the experienced angler, too, if necessary—will learn to tie the relatively few knots that follow, he should have little difficulty enjoying himself in most fishing situations. Later, should he find himself specializing in some particular type of fishing— perhaps trolling a certain natural bait for a specific ocean game fish, for instance—he can then learn how to tie the knots that have proven best for that particular phase of the sport. I suggest that you practice tying the following knots with light nylon rope, or heavy cord of a type that does not unravel easily—for such materials are easier to work than fishing line.

Line End Knot

Whether you use a simple hand line, wound on a frame, or a reel of some kind, you should prudently anchor the end. If not, should a fish take all of your line, the end will slip off the spool and disappear before you can grab it to hold on!

A simple yet effective knot for securing the end of a line used for bait casting or spinning—or the backing line on a fly reel—to the reel spool is shown in *Figure 2-1*. After the line has been looped about the spool it is tied back upon itself as shown, using a single overhand type knot. The second such knot, made in the end of the line, is to provide a means of preventing the end from slipping through the first knot when the line is drawn down tightly upon the spool.

Figure 2–1 Line End Knot

Improved Clinch Knot

After passing the end of your line, or leader, through the eye of the hook (or swivel), wind the line back upon itself, making at least five turns, all in the same direction, as shown in *Figure 2–2*. (Make only

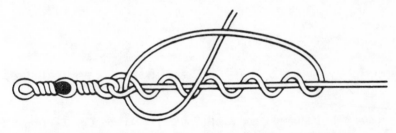

Figure 2–2 Improved Clinch Knot (Courtesy of Orvis Co.)

three turns, and you may decrease the knot's holding ability by as much as 40 per cent!)

Next, pass the end back through the first loop behind the eye, then also back through the larger loop you have just formed. Finally, pull the twists up tightly against the hook eye, by pulling slowly on the free end. Trim off this end, leaving about an eighth inch of line protruding.

Some anglers prefer to use the original version of this knot, called the "clinch knot," as shown in *Figure 2–3*. This knot is tied in a similar manner, save that when the end of the line is passed back through the first loop behind the eye, it is left there—omitting the extra tuck—before drawing the knot up tight. If you prefer to tie

Figure 2–3   Clinch Knot (Courtesy of Orvis Co.)

the original knot, I suggest that you first tie a simple overhand knot in the line end, as shown by the dotted lines, before drawing the knot down tight. This additional knot will prevent the end from slipping out through the twists.

Blood Knot

This efficient knot (see *Figure 2–4*) is a favorite for joining mono-filament lines of different diameters—for example, to make sections of

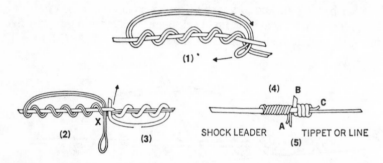

Figure 2–4   Improved Blood Knot (Courtesy of Du Pont Co.) For tying a heavy monofilament shock leader to a lighter monofilament line or tippet. (Two greatly uneven diameters of monofilament.)

(1) Double a sufficient length of the smaller diameter line so it can be wrapped around the standing part of the larger diameter line with at least five turns. Place the doubled end down between the strands.

(2) Hold the looped line between the thumb and the forefinger at the point marked X to keep from unwinding.

(3) Now wind the larger diameter line around the standing part of the doubled line three times, but in the opposite direction. Insert the end upward through the loop at the same point marked X.

(4) Pull the knot up slowly and tightly to keep it from slipping. Use the fingernails to push the loops together, if necessary.

(5) Now cut off the ends of the doubled loop (A) and the end of the heavy line (B), both about a quarter inch from the knot. Cut off the loose end of the doubled line (C) about a quarter inch from the knot.

a tapered fly rod leader. Should one of these two lines be considerably smaller than the other, tie an "improved" blood knot by using a doubled-back length of the smaller line—in the same manner as shown for the single line—to tie this knot.

You might say that this knot is actually two unimproved clinch knots, with the ends of each passed back through the center opening, in opposite directions, before pulling both the ends alternately tight. Be sure to wrap each about the opposite line five times before doing this. Finish by pulling with even pressure on both main lines simultaneously, thereby snubbing the wraps tightly together. Snip off both ends.

For those persons who have difficulty in keeping the end(s) in place, inside the center opening, prior to pulling tight the coils, a good trick is to tie the ends together *first*. (A simple overhand knot will suffice.) Then push them both down through the opening at the same time, as shown in *Figure 2–5*, and finish the knot in the usual manner.

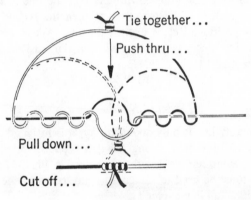

Figure 2–5

End Loop

Some lures—notably plugs—will not perform properly, regardless how hard one may try with rod tip and reel winding to bring out their best action, should the line or leader be knotted snugly to the lure eye. What is needed, instead, is an end loop that will permit the lure to swing freely, to dart and wiggle naturally through the water when it is retrieved. This applies, particularly, should the lure be of the type that has the action built in.

There are several methods for tying such a loop. The knot shown in *Figure 2–6* is simple and effective. Tie a single overhand knot to

Figure 2–6

form a small loop about six inches from the end of the line or leader. Pass the end of the line through the eye of the hook, or lure, then back through the loop first formed. Now use the free end of the line to tie a second overhand knot, this time forming a second small loop, this one on the fishing rod side of the first.

Finally, draw the first knot down tight over the line to form a loop about half an inch in diameter. Then tighten the second knot carefully, so it is positioned close against the first. When properly tied, this knot provides an end loop that will not tighten itself against the eye under strain.

Nail and Needle Knots

The average fly line is only about thirty yards in length, not nearly long enough to prevent a strong fish from pulling it all from the reel. Hence a considerable length of protective line—"backing," as it is called—must be used to safeguard against loss of the fly line, as is explained in detail in Chapter 11.

The knot used to join the fly line to its backing—and later, the fly line to its leader—should be one that permits these two junctions to pass through the rod guides with least resistance. Obviously, should an outward-racing line suddenly hang up against a guide, the guide —and likely several others, too—could be torn away. In fact, the rod might even break!

I have yet to find a knot that is completely "bump-free" for either use. Probably the closest a flycaster can come to such perfection is to whip-finish either a nail or a needle knot used at these two critical positions. That is, to wrap the knot with nylon thread, or perhaps dental floss, after which the joint is smoothed over with an application of liquid cement. (Pliobond is a good brand to use for this purpose, since this cement does not harden completely.)

The nail knot, shown in *Figure 2–7,* is tied with a nail, or similar shaped object. The nail is used to insure space to push the leader back through the several knot wraps, before these loops are drawn down tightly against the two lines, to finish the knot. Some flymen prefer to use a small tube, instead, to provide an easier return path for pushing the leader end back through.

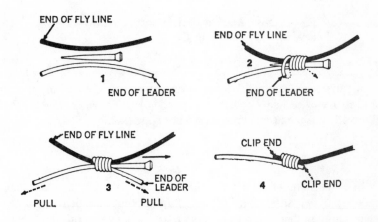

Figure 2–7 The Nail Knot (Courtesy of Orvis Co.) The nail knot is used to tie the butt end of your leader to the forward end of your fly line. It is also used to tie backing to a fly line. This knot gives a smooth, streamlined connection and the flat-lying knot will move freely through the guides of your rod, and if tied properly this knot cannot slip, cut or pull out. This knot is tied using either a tapered nail or piece of small tubing. Here's how to tie it: Hold the line, leader and tapered nail or tubing alongside each other as shown in (1). Allow ample overlap. Then wind leader downward around nail or tubing, line and itself six times, and run end of leader back along nail or through tubing up under loops, (2). Pull both ends of leader tight. Slip knot down nail or tubing, tightening by pulling both ends of leader as it goes. Slip nail or tubing out and retighten by again pulling leader ends, (3). Finally, pull line and leader tight and clip end of line and leader close to knot, (4).

Since a fly fisherman is apt to misplace both a nail or a small tube
—yet nearly always carries a long-shanked hook as part of his tackle
—such a hook can also be conveniently used to tie this knot, as
shown in *Figure 2–8*.

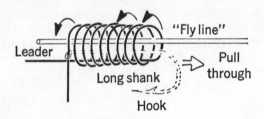

Figure 2–8 Another Nail Knot (Courtesy of
Sevenstrand Tackle Mfg. Co.)

A variation of the nail knot, and one easier to tie, especially if one
makes use of a handy tool like the Orvis Fly Threader used in the
illustration, is the needle knot shown in *Figure 2–9*.

In conclusion, let me caution that a poorly chosen or tied knot can
reduce the overall strength of your fishing outfit as much as 50 per
cent. On the other hand, exhaustive tests made by several line manufacturers indicate that a properly tied knot can maintain 90 per
cent, or more, of the original line strength. So don't be careless.
Practice until you have mastered the knots discussed here. Although
comparatively few in number, these will serve you well in practically
all fishing situations.

Don't hurry. Pull each knot carefully down into its finished state.
Don't trim the loose ends too closely. Finally, give the knot a last close
inspection before use—for it could be your last chance to do this.

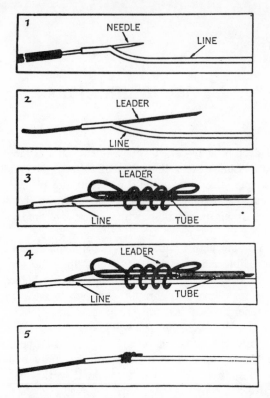

Figure 2–9 Needle Knot. Certainly the slick way to attach leader to fly line (or fly line to nylon backing).

(1) Take the needle (and red tube) from its hiding place in the reverse end of your Orvis Fly Threader.

(2) Slide the red tube off the needle, and run the point of the needle up through the center of the fly line, and out one side. Then draw it back free.

(3) Poke the leader up the hole made by the needle, up through the line core and out one side. It helps if your leader point has been cut on the bias, to give it a point.

(4) Lay the red tube and leader up along the fly line, wind the leader around line and leader and tube . . . bring leader end back and run it up through the tube under the loops you have just made.

(5) Withdraw the tube from under the loops and off the end of the leader. Pull up the turns snug, being careful not to let loops overlap each other if you want nice smooth appearance. Trim off end of nylon closely. (Courtesy of Orvis Co.)

Chapter 3
Using Natural Baits

There is a deep-rooted—and justified—belief among anglers that a natural bait is usually better than an artificial one. When all else fails —and sometimes after waiting until no critics are present to observe —the frustrated fisherman will bait his hook with a live minnow or crab, perhaps tip his artificial lure with a piece of shrimp, or other tidbit that will hopefully attract a fish.

There is nothing wrong with this. After all, the object is to bring home some edible meat, particularly when this has been promised. Wives can be devastating when told only minutes before mealtime that the plan for dinner has abruptly changed. What is wrong, however, is the belief that just because you lower a likely looking chunk or strip of bait into the water some fish will grab it.

Several considerations are involved here, not all of them always under the angler's control. For reasons still not fully understood by man, fish—like other creatures in the animal world—may suddenly become active and start to feed. I have observed this phenomenon repeatedly. You may be drifting lazily across a wide estuarine bay in your silent outboard skiff. Nothing is biting. Not even a crab scuttles across the bottom.

The sun is warm against the back of your neck; the light salt breeze is a gentle kiss against your cheek. You feel drowsy.

Abruptly, several gulls appear from nowhere and land lightly upon a partially exposed sand bar nearby. The birds wade out expectantly into the shallows, where the water—calm as a mirror surface only moments before—now reveals slight boils and wakes.

Farther out, a small school of bait fish may break nervously from the surface, pursued there by some larger fish that remains unseen. Perhaps you have grown tired of fruitlessly casting your streamer fly —and now a sea trout or snook lunges eagerly at the tiny offering of hair and feathers as it trails haphazardly astern, on the surface . . .

The marine world has suddenly come alive. Sometimes, even when you can't observe it thus, you can feel it. It can be an exciting feeling, indeed! For now—until such time as it abruptly stops again—this "feeding period" likely will produce one frenzied strike after another. The fish may grab practically anything you choose to throw at them!

What has brought about this exciting change? What, indeed. A changing tide, wind direction, barometric pressure, water temperature, the sudden stirring—perhaps appearance—of bait—these are some of the things that can launch a feeding period. No man has yet been able to use such variables in a foolproof equation to predict when fish will and will not bite.

I know dedicated anglers—so-called "purists"—who rarely use natural bait, yet who can usually outfish those who do use it. To observe this being done can be misleading, however. Nearly always, close examination will reveal that the natural bait fisherman in such competitions has been using the wrong kind of bait, or has failed to present it properly.

Personally, I prefer to use artificials. It gives me more satisfaction, a greater thrill of achievement, to fool a fish with a phony bait than it does to catch him with a real offering. Too, I don't like to see large quantities of natural bait—most of it caught by commercial netters—used up. Continue to remove such natural food and you end up with fewer game fish.

There is nothing—nothing—that can consistently appeal more to a hungry fish than a natural food upon which he has grown accustomed to feeding. When the man using an artificial bait continues to catch the most fish, it is usually traceable to the fact that the other angler has hooked his live minnow, or other natural bait, in such a manner that it cannot swim and move naturally, thereby inviting the suspicion of the watching bass or other fish. Or perhaps the bait is old, hence does not have an appealing smell; and so on.

The first step when using natural bait, therefore, is to determine what natural food is being fed upon by the fish. Then use this same food as bait. An ideal way to do this is to inspect the stomach contents of a fish of the type you want to catch. Should this not prove possible, try to learn from other anglers what type of bait works best in the area involved. If for some reason this information is not available, you must decide for yourself—and the wrong decision can cost you a poor day of fishing.

NATURAL BAITS FOR FRESHWATER

Minnows

There are over a hundred kinds of minnows in fresh water—and anglers have probably used these to catch that many different kinds of fish—bass, especially. So bait a tiny hook (about a No. 16) and see if you cannot catch some of these little fish, to be used alive for bait. Or, better, use a minnow trap. If you have not brought some bread, or some cooked or raw meat, along to use for minnow bait, turn over a rock or log and find worms or insects.

The baited trap should be placed on the bottom of stream or lake. (Such traps can be purchased.) Minnows can also be dipped at times from shallow water with a fine-meshed hand net. In Florida, saltwater fishermen hurl a casting net over surfaced schools of minnows and other small bait fish (see *Photo 8*).

Once caught, the minnows should be kept alive inside a perforated bait bucket (which may also be purchased). This bucket may be kept overboard, so a flow of water can move freely through it, for minnows require a lot of oxygen to remain alive. Some buckets, however, are equipped with a small pump, to aerate the water, and this permits them to be used on land, or in a boat. Otherwise, you must change the bucket water repeatedly. Be careful when you do this not to dump out the fish, too.

Minnows may be hooked in different ways, depending upon whether you wish to use them live or dead. Live minnows are used most for still fishing; dead ones, for casting and trolling.

It is best to fish a live minnow without float or sinker, if you can. Pay out just enough line so the little fish can swim down to a position just above the bottom, where it can be readily seen by the larger fish that habitually prowl there. (Give the minnow more line than this, and it will very likely hide itself in bottom grass, or elsewhere, for protection.) For this kind of fishing the minnow should be hooked through either the tail, or through the fleshy portion of the back—crosswise—between dorsal fin and backbone, as shown in *Figure 3–1*. (Do not injure the backbone with the hook.)

Should current, or other conditions, make it difficult for the little

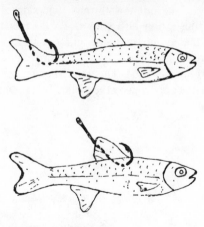

Figure 3–1

swimmer to remain near the bottom while you are still-fishing, crimp a small split-shot, or several if necessary, over the line, a couple feet or so above the fish. A small surface float may prove necessary, too, to position the minnow properly. Some live minnow anglers use a deep-trolling rig with a bank, or other rounded, sinker that bumps along the bottom. The forward-moving minnow, meanwhile, is kept suspended just above the bottom by a small submerged ball float. This bobber is fastened only a foot or so above the live bait.

A dead minnow to be used for still fishing, casting or trolling can be hooked through both lips, as shown in *Figure 3–2*. Some fisher-

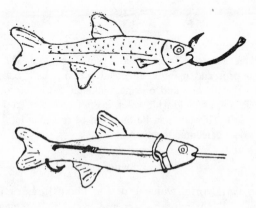

Figure 3–2

men prefer to hook the minnow through one side of the body, near the tail, as the illustration also shows. To do this the barb is first passed through the mouth and one gill opening, with the line or leader then secured behind the head with a simple hitch, to insure that the bait will be trolled headfirst. The unbalancing position of the hook, since it is on one side only, causes the trolled bait to wiggle invitingly.

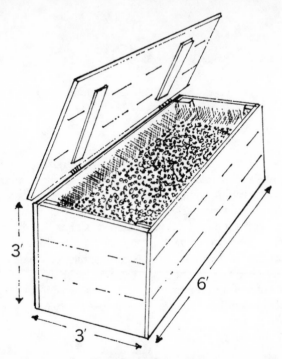

Figure 3–3 Worm Storage Box (Capacity: 300 adult worms.) Roof is used only when protection from sun and rain is required. The bed mixture can be loam, peat and manure, in equal proportions. FOOD: Mix three pounds of meal with one and one half pounds shortening or lard (used kitchen fat will do) and add with water, every two weeks, to the top twelve inches of the soil. This box can be built out of two-inch lumber or bricks or concrete blocks cemented together.

Worms

The lowly earthworm, which grows to about three or four inches, makes a good bait for panfish, bass and trout. This angleworm is encountered in gardens, in fields and forests where soil is rich and moist. (A related type of worm, one that is usually slimmer and red, instead of pink, prefers compost piles.) A considerably larger version of the earthworm, the so-called night crawler, is about twice as big. It is named thus because it likes to come out of the earth after dark, usually atop moist grass.

Worms should be dug beforehand, then kept in a suitable container until fishing time. Dedicated worm fishermen prefer to build a permanent (home) box of wood to store such bait. (A representative size would be 1×1×2 feet—see *Figure 3–3*—although I've seen them thrice that size.) A small styrofoam bucket or similar container may be used to carry afield the daily fishing supply.

The home box is filled about halfway with rich soil, grass, leaves, etc., into which the captured worms quickly dig. The box should be kept in the shade, and can be lidless if protected from the rain. Some wormers like to add coffee grounds, meal and various other materials to insure fat, healthy worms. Others prefer to purchase such food and bedding materials ready-mixed in small bags.

Figure 3–4 illustrates how several worms can be attached to a

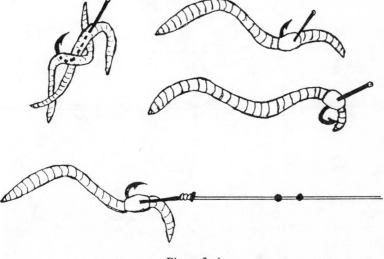

Figure 3–4

single hook when necessary (i.e., when they are small), also how one large worm can be rigged—weedless and otherwise—for still fishing and trolling. Note how one or more small (shot) sinkers can be used to send the worm bottomward, when necessary.

Avoid fishing a dead worm. To keep it alive, so it will continue to appeal to the most fish, use the smallest hook possible, pierced through the worm's "collar," as shown. Like minnows, worms do attract a variety of fish, notably panfish.

Crayfish

Crayfish, also called crawfish and crawdads, resemble miniature lobsters. They are usually only three inches, or less, in length. Depending upon their size, crayfish make fine bait when used for panfish, bass (especially), pike, muskellunge and other species. The meat is sometimes removed from the shell to make catfish bait.

These little two-clawed crustaceans live both in and out of the water. Anglers dig crayfish from small holes along stream and lake

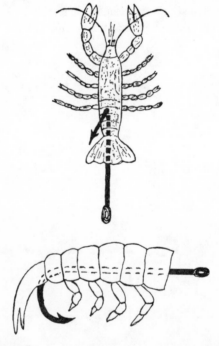

Figure 3–5

shores (they come out mostly after dark) and dislodge them from be-neath submerged stones and other bottom objects, in the shallows. In either case a small dip net will prove handy. For a disturbed crayfish can move quickly beyond reach. On land they usually run backwards.

Crayfish can be kept alive in a bucket of clean fresh water while you are fishing. Some anglers prefer to add grass or a few aquatic plants to the water. To keep a crayfish alive on your hook, pierce the barb through its tail—not the body—as shown in *Figure 3–5*.

It is a good idea first to remove the two large claws. Even then, the little fellow will crawl stubbornly along the bottom, looking for a place under, or inside, which to hide. So avoid slack line; try to fish this live bait just above the bottom.

Crayfish shed their shells periodically as they grow. A crayfish in the soft state makes an excellent bait. But to keep it on the hook, it should be wrapped fast with thread. Or use a rubber band.

To use a dead crayfish, simply remove the head, then slide the body over the hook, as shown.

Frogs

These do not seem to be as widely used as they once were, although a live frog is hard to beat for taking a big bass (especially after dark) or a musky or northern pike. Perhaps the current crop of anglers were not taught by fishing parents, as youngsters once were, how to find and catch frogs in meadows and grassy marshes, and along stream and pond banks.

Or perhaps today's fisherman is squeamish about the usual practice of hooking a live frog through the upper muscle of a rear leg, for still fishing, or through both lips, to keep the mouth closed and prevent drowning, as shown in *Figure 3–6*. (This last rig is best for casting.)

The frog does look pretty pathetic when this is done to him. Tackle stores, however, sell a harness inside which a live frog can be placed, and still serve effectively as a bait. Too, some concerned anglers attach the frog to the hook with rubber bands.

Immature frogs—even those as small as tadpoles—play an impor-tant role in catching fish when lip or tail hooked. The size of the frog is more important than the several species that are normally avail-able: you should choose a big mouthful of frog for an anticipated big musky, for example, or a smaller frog for a smaller fish. The trick is to

Figure 3–6

let the frog swim naturally in its customary habitat of lily pads, along grassy shorelines, etc. Use a weedless hook when necessary.

Frogs may be kept at the fishing site inside a bait bucket partly filled with moist grass or moss. Should it become necessary to use a dead frog, use the lip-hooked method and try to swim the offering back naturally during the retrieve. That is, with the jerky (kick and plunge forward) movement of the submerged frog. Skittering a bait over grass and lily pads can also drive muskies and bass wild.

Salamanders

These small (three- to seven-inch) amphibians resemble lizards. In fact, they are called "spring lizards" in some areas.

There are many kinds, both upland and water-frequenting varieties. Look for them especially around moist areas, under stones and similar hiding places. They are very quick.

Bass, trout and catfish love salamanders. Probably the best place to hook one of these little creatures is through both lips, since the tail is easily shed. An alternative position, as shown in *Figure 3–7*, would

Figure 3–7

be through the body. But this works best when fishing this bait dead.

Like frogs, salamanders can be carried in a bait bucket, with grass.

Grasshoppers and Crickets

Fish feed upon three main types of food in fresh water. Two of these types we have already discussed in part: that food which habitually swims below the surface, like minnows, for example, and the kind that occasionally moves across the surface, like frogs and salamanders. A third type is that which may fall into the water accidentally, or is carried there by the wind, etc. Included in this last category are grasshoppers and crickets.

Grasshoppers are the more sturdy of the two, for hooking purposes, but both are fragile. Try to hook each carefully under its collar, if you wish to keep it alive (which is best), or use wraps of black thread, or a rubber band, to hold fast the bait to the hook, as shown in *Figure 3–8*.

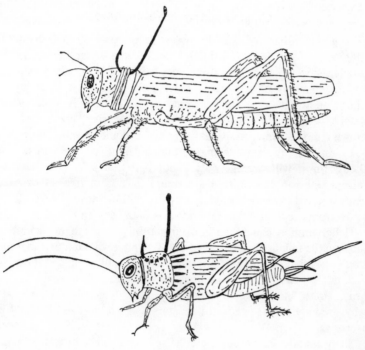

Figure 3–8

A small dip, or butterfly-catching type, net can be used to capture 'hoppers, especially from midsummer on, in gardens, grassy fields, on stream banks and along the edges of backcountry roads. Early morning is a good time for this. Crickets are best found under rocks, logs, brush and similar hiding places, since they come out mostly after dark.

A good way to fish both these baits is simply to float the insect away across the surface, particularly near a shoreline, as if the grasshopper or cricket had fallen in. If it should sink helplessly, that's natural, too. Few fresh water panfish and game fish, indeed, can resist such an offering when other feeding conditions are right.

There are many terrestrial (earth-living) insects like 'hoppers and crickets and dragonflies, and what not, that may sooner or later drop into water, to provide a tasty tidbit for some alert fish. Even a mouse may fall in and be promptly gobbled up (which is why we use artificial lures that resemble mice).

Other Insects and Natural Foods

A great number of aquatic insects spend part of their lives submerged, hence provide fish food. Consider the hellgrammite, for example, which often makes a fine bass bait, and is usually good, also, for all members of the pike family. This aquatic larva, or nymph (i.e., the wingless, wormlike form) of the dobsonfly is the newly hatched insect before it undergoes metamorphosis. That is, before it crawls from the water to sprout wings and become an actual fly.

In time a hellgrammite may attain a length of three inches, although most will average only about half that size. Few bass and other game fish can resist this creature that looks like an oversized centipede, when it is floated innocently within range. For such fish know from experience that this morsel is both tasty and helpless.

Hellgrammites should be hooked carefully beneath the collar, or through the tail, as shown in *Figure 3–9*. And it will be found that they stay in position on the barb quite well. Use a small hook, about No. 14.

Similarly, the larvae or nymphs of such other flies as the caddis, May, stone, etc., provide good natural fish baits—which explains why so many of our artificial flies (lures) resemble these hatched insect eggs.

Such aquatic larvae can be collected by turning over stones and other bottom objects in shallow water, and using a fine-mesh dip net

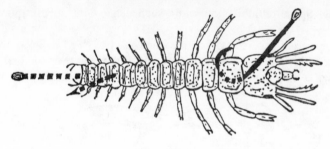

Figure 3–9

to trap the thus dislodged nymphs. If there is a current, a piece of fine window screen may be positioned on the down-current side to catch the drifting larvae.

Caterpillars, grubs (the larvae of beetles), as well as certain beetles themselves (the Japanese, the June bug, etc.) can also be used effectively as bait for panfish, bass, walleyes and other fish. Look for these baits in the garden, inside rotten stumps, under tree bark, etc. Ask local anglers where to look, if you don't know. You may have to thread-wrap such fragile baits, or secure them to the hook with rubber bands. Try to run the hook carefully under the skin of the grub.

The familiar small, multi-compartment plastic lure box, with its sliding lid, provides a convenient means for carrying afield crickets, grasshoppers, hellgrammites and similar small natural baits. Moist grass, leaves, etc., can be added to provide both food and bedding.

Dead Baits for Fresh Water

It may not always be possible, of course, to provide yourself live fish, amphibians or insects with which to bait your hook. To safeguard against this possibility, you can carry with you to the fishing site dead bait in the form of pickled pork rind (it is usually easier to buy a small jar of the commercially prepared kind), salmon eggs, doughballs, shrimp (the fresh water kind). And, of course, in dead condition any of the minnows, crayfish, frogs, eels, clams and mussels, home-grown mealworms, etc., that we have, or have not, already discussed. As you become seriously involved with fishing you will discover there are many kinds of live and dead natural baits. Over a hundred kinds of the former have been listed for fresh water bass alone! Space prohibits going into such detail here, so ask questions locally.

A piece of tapered pork rind, when used to "tip" a jig, spoon or other artificial lure (use the widest end of the rind over the barb; see *Figure 3–10*) can provide a very effective bait, especially for black

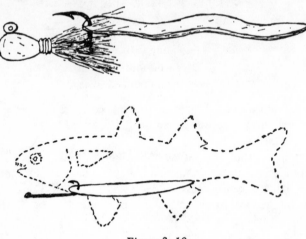

Figure 3–10

bass. This supple tail will undulate in tantalizing manner, with even the slightest forward movement of the hook. A similar effect can be achieved, with such a lure, by cutting a strip of white-skinned flesh from the belly of a perch or other fish (often an unwanted carp, sucker, etc.) and using this in connection with a hook only, no artificial lure. This narrow "strip" bait may be from two to four inches (or longer) in length, and should vary proportionately in width—from about ⅜ to ⅝ inch, for the figures used here—depending upon its length. Pierce the barb but once, through the widest end.

Some fishermen prefer to leave the bottom fins on such a bait, to improve its swimming action. Others like to scrape away the flesh from the rear inch, or so, of the strip. This leaves only the skin there, to undulate more freely, because of the increased thinness. And there are those anglers who cut a twin-tailed strip, instead of a single one, to double the movement of the nearly closed "V" thus formed.

Bottom fishermen are often content simply to cut a small chunk of such fish bait to be impaled upon the hook.

Salmon eggs are simply that: eggs that have been salvaged—or taken—for bait use, rather than allowed to produce young fish. This bait can be deadly, especially upon trout and char, which feed largely upon such eggs, inasmuch as swallowing the egg invariably means swallowing the hook, too. I have fished for rainbows in the Big Salmon region of Alaska's Katmai Peninsula—perhaps the greatest salmon spawning area in the world. There I have seen these and other trout gorge themselves upon the single eggs, sometimes the clusters, that are swept from the salmon breeding nests by the current.

Thus a single egg allowed to tumble downstream, impaled upon a short-shanked hook that has been matched in size to the egg's diameter, can prove most effective. The eggs are fragile, of course, and should be positioned upon the hook carefully, using the steps shown in *Photo 31*. This illustration also shows how a terminal rig with egg type sinker can be used, to insure that the bait is left free to be moved easily by a current; and how a cluster of eggs can be secured to a hook. (Anglers sometimes use small egg sacs to hold the cluster to the hook.)

Doughball bait is easily prepared, and keeps well. But it can be washed off the hook. It seems to be effective mostly with catfish, bullheads, carp and similar species that are not high on the game fish list, but which do provide considerable sport.

There are dozens of possible doughball recipes, with unyielding supporters of each. Some of these "mixtures" call for cheese; others, for meat, food extracts, etc. Sometimes the meat is first purposely allowed to rot (clams left in the sun, for instance) to provide a strong, hopefully fish-attracting stench.

In any event, a bread dough, or paste, usually serves as the base. This should be molded carefully about the hook, before using, and it should be firm enough to remain there a reasonable time. To make the dough, soak several crumbled slices of bread in water—inside a small cheesecloth sack, even a folded handkerchief, if necessary. Squeeze the contents as dry as possible, by hand, then mix in enough cornmeal to make the desired dough consistency. (Use too much meal and the dough will become too brittle; it will break away from the hook.)

Then fish this bait on the bottom. Move it as little as possible, to make it last longer.

Natural Baits for Salt Water

In the oceans, estuarine bays, salt rivers and creeks it is usually best to use a local fish, either alive or dead, for bait. The fish may be attached to the hook(s) whole—its size determined by the size of the larger fish to be caught—or it can be cut, instead, into inviting strips and chunks.

Popular, also, for saltwater baits are shrimps, crabs, eels and squid. Used less often, perhaps, but still quite effectively, are clams and mussels, bloodworms, sandworms and sand fleas. Insects and amphibians are not saltwater baits.

Some saltwater fish have sharp teeth—perhaps even keen-edged tail ridges and bony gill covers—that can cut quickly through an ordinary line. So it may prove necessary to employ a shock leader—one that has a breaking strength (diameter) greater than that of the line, as was explained in Chapter 1.

Using a Whole Fish

Fish that may be used for natural bait come in a variety of sizes, shapes and species in salt water: fingerling mullet, pilchards, killifish, balao and silversides (spearing), to name some of the smaller ones. In the fall, when the first northeasters begin to blow in Florida, where I live, one is apt to see great schools of fingerling mullet moving slowly southward along the Atlantic coast, close against the shore. It is not unusual to observe one of these dark patches that move slowly across the sea's surface suddenly erupt into a boiling froth— sometimes an acre in size—as hundreds of frenzied little bait fish leap into the air in a futile effort to escape the attack of bluefish, mackerel, snook and other foraging predators underneath.

I have seen the ocean beach littered with countless silversides— delicate little bait fish struggling helplessly, high up on the dry portion of the beach—driven there by hungry bluefish and other gamesters. All one need do under such happy fishing conditions is to pick up one of these wriggling bait fish, pierce it with a hook, and cast it out a few feet into the surf. Nearly always, one of the excited blues darting expectantly to and fro there will nail your offering as soon as it strikes the water.

As might be expected, there are an infinite number of uses for live bait—whole fish, both large and small—and to list the potential of each is, of course, beyond the capability of this book. Once again I must urge you to inquire of local anglers what species have been found best, and how these are rigged. In Florida, for example, the little pinfish (sailor's choice) makes an excellent live bait, particularly for tarpon, amberjack, spinner sharks, grouper and cobia.

To keep any size of fish alive, as bait, at the end of your line, it can be hooked either through the lips, or through the fleshy portion of the back, as shown in *Figure 3–2*, for fresh water minnows. To make sure of not striking the backbone, some saltwater anglers prefer to secure the barb alongside this critical bone, instead of passing over it.

When using a fish alive, the idea—of course—is to let the bait swim naturally, along the edges of reefs, down into the deeper holes that are often found in shoal areas, and so on. To do this, avoid using a weighted terminal rig that is so heavy it hinders the natural action of the bait fish. In fact, use no sinker at all, if you can do without one.

A live eel, for example, can be a very effective bait for striped bass and other saltwater fish. Similarly, a tarpon or big snook will find it hard to resist a live mullet that crosses its path. And live mackerel have proven great baits for big stripers, and tuna.

To rig a live eel you will have first to grasp the slippery creature firmly with a dry towel, perhaps a burlap sack, then hook it through one side of its mouth, or through the eyes, using a snap swivel right at the hook, as shown in *Figure 3–11*. The swivel will help prevent the line-twisting for which eels are notorious.

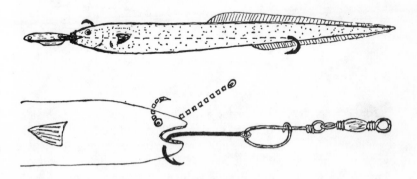

Figure 3–11

A mackerel, eel, mullet or other fish can also be used whole after it is dead, of course. In fact, many anglers prefer to handle a dead bait, especially for trolling. A dead (and now docile) eel, for example, requires only that a long bait-rigging needle be thrust into its mouth, down through two thirds of the body, to emerge on the underside for positioning there a downturned hook that will work in conjunction with a second, or upturned, hook at the head that is part of a metal (block tin) squid, as shown in *Figure 3–11*. The metal squid provides the weight needed for keeping the eel down while trolling.

Again, a whole, dead "ballyhoo" (balao) rigged as shown in *Figure 3–12* is ideal for trolling—not only for sailfish, white marlin and

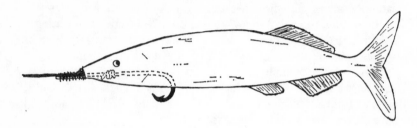

Figure 3–12

other surface species—but also for snapper, grouper and other so-called bottom species when this bait is trolled deep over reefs, and in channels and cuts, using a keel sinker as shown in *Figure 3–13*.

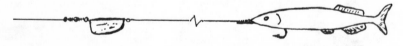

Figure 3–13

Strip and Cut Baits

Any fish can be cut to provide either fillets (strips) from each side, usually a total of four of these, or simply chunks of meat to be pierced by a hook. The chunks are usually used for bottom fishing. The strip, when it is trolled behind a moving boat, will undulate invitingly through the water, simulating the swimming action of a bait fish. It behaves this way, too, when it is cast out and retrieved by an angler remaining in one spot.

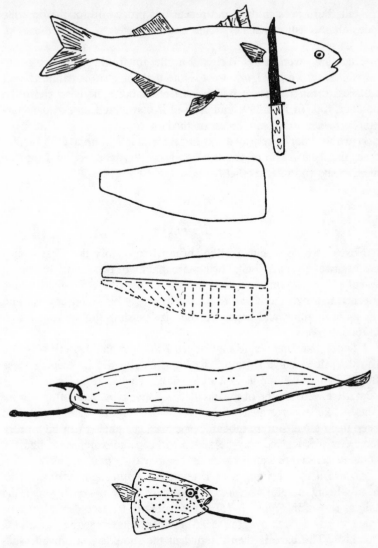

Figure 3–14

To fillet a fish for bait, lay it flat upon a table or other surface. Then, using a sharp long-bladed knife, make an entry slit—approximately at right angles to the backbone—just behind the head, as shown in *Figure 3–14*. Finally, keeping the blade flat against the backbone, slice away half the fish as you move the blade back toward the tail. Turn the fish over and repeat this procedure for the opposite side. (If the fish has scales, some anglers prefer to scrape these off, first.)

There are several ways to rig a fish fillet for trolling use. One popular way is shown in *Figure 3–14*. Note that the strip is trimmed so it will pass through the water with least resistance. The head can often be used, too. In Florida a mullet head is considered an excellent tarpon bait when fished motionless on the bottom.

A whole fillet may prove too large for small bottom fish. In that case, simply use one of the smaller pieces that can be cut from the fillet, as shown in *Figure 3–14*.

Shrimp

Next to whole or cut fish the shrimp is probably the most widely used saltwater natural bait. Shrimp are mainly of two kinds: the small, so-called "grass" shrimp (that can be caught with a fine-mesh seine, dip net or towed mesh bag trap used in grassy bays and creeks) and the more familiar, and larger, "eating-size" shrimp that are purchased in food markets.

I doubt that any single bait appeals to a greater variety of game fish than does a live shrimp. The big difficulty lies in keeping these fragile baits alive for use on other days. They fare quite well in a boat's live well, if it be of the circulating water type. A floating shrimp "car"—like a perforated bucket suspended in the water—will also keep them alive. But an inboard, or bank, bait bucket can be a problem, even though ice may be added to keep the water cool, and the contents aerated repeatedly with oxygen-releasing tablets.

To fish a live shrimp, hook it once, either through the top of the head—being careful to *miss* the dark spot there—or through the tail, as shown in *Figure 3–15*. If the bait is to be used dead, it is customary first to remove the head (it can hinder setting the hook quickly). The barb is then inserted at the shoulder, meanwhile sliding the shrimp carefully down over the hook in such a manner that its now curving body covers most, if not all, the hook shank, as shown in *Figure 3–16*.

If the shrimp are of small size, two can be impaled upon the same hook.

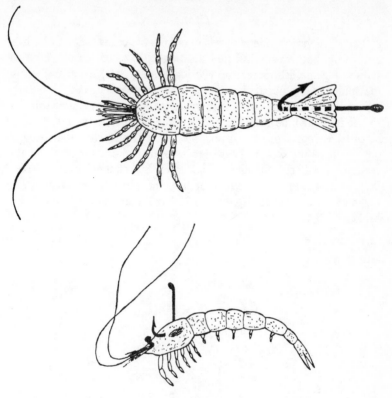

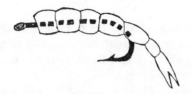

Figure 3–15

Figure 3–16

Crabs

There are various kinds of easily obtainable crabs that can be used effectively, both in the live and dead state, to catch various kinds of saltwater game fish. Some top Florida Keys guides, for example, use the spider crab—about the size of a twenty-five-cent coin—to catch record-size permit, one of the otherwise most wary of all game fish.

The familiar blue crab, the one with the wicked claws that is a table favorite, is found in salt—sometimes even fresh—shallows throughout much of the world. There are several methods for hooking this crab so it will remain alive—and catch big channel bass, stripers, kingfish and many other kinds of fish, including tarpon—but I like the method shown in *Figure 3–17*. Note that the large claws are broken off before use.

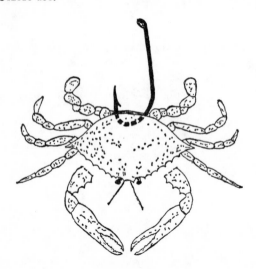

Figure 3–17

A soft-shell blue, or "shedder" crab (one that has recently shed its hard shell) can prove even more effective. It is so soft, however, that if it is to be used whole, it may be necessary to secure it to the hook with thread, or rubber bands.

The smaller calico, or lady, crab that is found usually buried in the sand, sometimes swimming in the surf backwash, along ocean beaches, resembles the blue crab in appearance. It can be hooked in the same manner as shown, and makes a good bait for channel and striped bass.

A hermit crab should be hooked first through the body, then through the tail, as shown in *Figure 3–18*, after first removing the

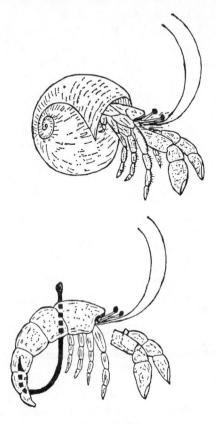

Figure 3–18

claws. These odd little fellows are found in tidal shallows, and along sand beaches, where they live inside empty shells that they have adopted. A hermit crab will live inside such a shell, carrying it about with him, until he finds another that he likes better. Then he will abandon the first and move into the other.

Your job is to get him out, and you may have to break the shell— if the heat from a close-held match fails to do the trick. Hermit crabs make excellent bait for bonefish, permit, sheepshead, blackfish and some other species, too.

The harmless fiddler crab is a fast-running little fellow who dodges nimbly out from underfoot when a human approaches. Meanwhile, he will wave his single claw aloft threateningly, like a musician holding up his violin. (Hence the name, fiddler.)

Fiddlers usually move in swarms, in the tide line areas, and make good bait for snapper, drum, redfish and others. They are also a superb sheepshead bait. The claw should be removed and the crab hooked through the body, as shown in *Figure 3–19*.

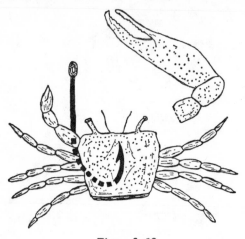

Figure 3–19

Sand Flea

This small, hard-shelled mole crab also serves as a good bait for a variety of saltwater fish, and especially for pompano. These energetic little diggers resemble a large egg sinker in size and shape and are found on ocean beaches, close to the surf. If you look closely, each time a wave breaks and recedes, you may—if you are lucky—see the sand flea's "whiskers" protruding slightly from the wet sand as it strains plankton from the disappearing water. These mole crabs can be scooped out of the sand by hand. A faster method, however, is to use a special rake that can be purchased or made. It employs a wire basket, usually made of quarter-inch galvanized mesh, that lets the sand pass through, yet retains the fleas.

Tackle stores and ocean pier bait shops often have sand fleas for sale. The strangely designed little creatures can be pierced by the hook from the rear, as shown in *Figure 3–20*.

They are also a good bait for drum, blackfish, bonefish, sheepshead, channel and striped bass, and kingfish. You may have to hook on more than one flea to attract the larger of these game fish.

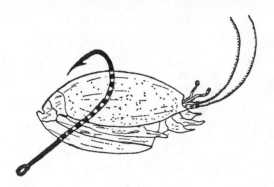

Figure 3–20

Squid and Octopodes

The squid is a miniature version of the equally harmless octopus— the so-called terrible "devilfish" of early sea legends. The popular, easy to purchase and use squid keeps well and works well as a bait for many kinds of saltwater fish, both the inshore and offshore kinds.

The firm white meat of the ten-armed squid is readily cut into strips or chunks, as may be needed, for trolling or still fishing. And the squid can be used whole to attract striped bass and other large fish, when it is rigged as shown in *Figure 3–21*.

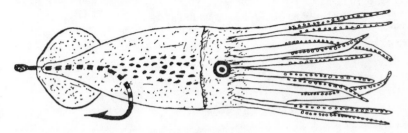

Figure 3–21

I know a Florida heavy-tackle angler who once held a dozen world fishing records at one time. One of his favorite baits is a baby octopus that weighs a pound or less. He finds these hiding at times inside drainpipes that empty rain runoff into a large estuarine bay. The eight-tentacled creature with the rounded, saclike body likes to find seclusion in such places.

Clams and Mussels

Bottom species like sea bass, blackfish and porgies have long been caught by baiting a hook with a piece of tongue, or foot, from a sea clam or one of the various other clams. As a boy I used to "tread-out" cherrystone clams (half-grown quahogs) with my feet, for example, in the muddy bottom of a wide and shallow New Jersey coastal bay—Barnegat—then proceed to catch flounders, weakfish and croakers with those of the tasty clams that I didn't consume myself, raw.

Mussels, too, can be used effectively for bait for these and other bottom fish in salt water. Mussels grow from rock jetties, pilings, etc., in coastal waters.

The trouble with both these mollusks is that nearly all the body is soft, hence difficult to keep on a hook. Some anglers wrap the clam or mussel against the hook, using thread. Others prefer to use these mollusks only for chum. (See Chapter 14.)

Bloodworms and Sandworms

These may be purchased in saltwater tackle and bait shops. They make good baits for kingfish, weakfish, flounders, striped bass, porgies and other ocean and estuarine fish—even eels (which, in turn, can then be used for bait themselves, as already described).

These worms may be hooked through the head, or mouth. Or, if you prefer to keep the worm alive, you can secure the head to a hook by means of rubber bands, as shown in *Figure 3–22.*

Figure 3–22.

Worms can be drifted out with the current—a very effective method for weakfish, particularly—or a three-way terminal rig can be employed that will allow the worm to float just above the bottom (see *Figure 3–23*) when slow-trolled from a drifting boat. This last method is a productive one for striped bass.

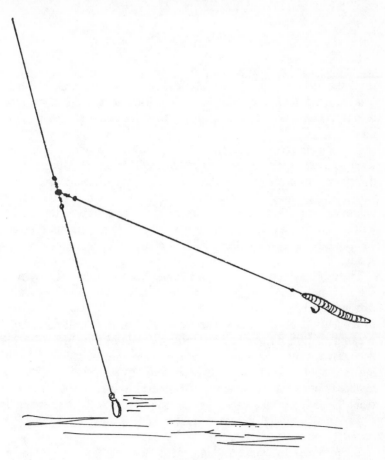

Figure 3–23

Chapter 4
Artificial Lures

An artificial object is something made by man, in imitation of something that occurs in nature. An artificial lure resembles a natural bait. It is intended to appear edible to a fish, so that he will bite down upon it, only to discover—hopefully, too late—that there is a hook in his mouth.

To play its role of deception successfully the artificial lure must meet several important requirements, practically all of which are the direct responsibility of the fisherman—the play director, as it were. First, the lure must occupy a position in the water where the intended victim can become aware of its presence. There is little point, for example, in using a floating lure to try and attract the attention of fish feeding far below, where there is small chance they will notice the offering.

The fish may become aware of the lure and still refuse it, however, should it not be of recognizable shape or satisfactory size. Generally, if trout are rising to feed upon a certain kind of fly, you will be wise to try and match that particular hatch. Again, if you are after large ocean game fish it is well to go by the old rule of thumb that "A big fish prefers a big mouthful." There are exceptions, of course, for fishing is a sport abounding with exceptions. I've repeatedly observed hundred-pound tarpon inhale tiny flies, for instance, in preference to much larger plugs and other conventional lures. A fly, remember, is a very small artificial lure: a hair, feather and tinsel imitation of an actual fly, or other small insect.

Color is also a consideration, but is not nearly so important as many fishermen mistakenly believe. True, there are those times when "They won't hit anything but yellow today—" (etc.). But it has been my experience that these are isolated instances.

What *is* of great importance, however, is the "action" of the lure: the way it moves through the water, under the guidance of the fisherman. A school of ravenous, excited bluefish or mackerel, for example, tearing up the sea's surface as they feed upon terrified bait fish, will strike best at a lure that darts and skips away before them—as if it, too, were attempting to escape. Conversely, a big—and hence nearly always lazy—fresh water black bass likely will not be tempted to leave his grassy bottom lair unless the deep-running lure that swims past does so in a wobbling, uncertain manner—perhaps resembling an injured minnow, to fool Mr. Bass into believing, here is a tasty morsel that he won't have to exercise himself much to catch.

Some lures have the action built in. That is, all the angler need do is subject the artificial to a steady retrieve, and it will swim toward him through the water in quite lifelike manner, undulating and wiggling enticingly en route. With other lures, however, one is obliged to twitch the rod tip, to vary the retrieve speed and generally try to impart lifelike motion to the lure as it moves.

Today's angler has available the greatest variety of artificial lures since fishing began. Before describing these I would like to make it clear that *no* lure can be depended upon consistently to catch fish, contrary to the claims of certain enthusiasts (the manufacturers, mainly). An artificial may work beautifully for you one day, only to fail miserably the following day, even though you fish in the same spot, at the same hour, with the same tackle and so on.

Don't ask me why this is so. As I pointed out in the preceding chapter, there are many variables involved in the fishing equation. I have met many anglers who claimed to have had the answer. But time invariably proved each one wrong. Men have spent years keeping faithful records based upon lure types, colors and other conditions under which they have caught certain kinds of fish—only to find, in the end, that such information was useful only in a general way. Let us be glad this is so. Were it not—were we able to catch all the fish we wanted, every time—the sport would soon lose its main appeal —which stems from its very uncertainty. Too, greedy men would soon succeed in hopelessly decimating the game fish population. They have already largely succeeded in doing this in many areas.

It is true that some *types* of artificial lures will consistently fall into certain broad categories of effectiveness. I believe that it can be claimed without dispute, for example, that the "jig"—the weighted-head lure, with its hook dressed with hair, feather or nylon skirt, which is probably the world's oldest artificial—consistently takes more fish, and continues to be sold more often, throughout the world, than any other lure. I know an angler who has used only a yellow, nylon-tailed type jig to land about 90 per cent of the many shallow water game fish that Florida offers. Again, so-called top water—or floating —plugs of the darter type have probably accounted for more large-mouth bass and snook than any other lure.

But there are many kinds of jigs and darters. My favorite darter happens to be a yellow-bodied, red and black spotted wooden plug made by Creek Chub Bait Company. I am convinced that, equipped with this one shallow-diving floater, I would never be obliged to starve—anywhere that fish swim in shallow water. However, I've seen other anglers fail with this fine plug, simply because they never learned how to impart properly the "cross-stitch" retrieve action that comes only with a proper combination of alternately reeling in and twitching the rod tip. So, you see, there can be no justification for me to recommend this particular lure as the consistent answer to any-one's fishing problems.

Plugs

Let's begin with the plug. (I wish someone would tell me how this lure got its odd name!) It is made either of wood or plastic, and is shaped to resemble a small fish upon which larger game fish feed. Again—hopefully—it will be designed to move through the water in an appealing, lifelike manner when retrieved.

I used the word "hopefully" since there continues to be much controversy over whether a fish sees, and recognizes, shapes and colors the way humans do. It would seem logical, for instance, to pursue bluefish and tarpon with a plug shaped and colored like a fingerling mullet, since both these species feed upon such small fish. But do these larger fish recognize such a lure solely as a mullet? Or do they merely associate the moving object, in a vague way, with something familiar and edible? I've caught bluefish in the surf with a strip of torn handkerchief on my hook—and I've taken tarpon on banana skins! A fresh water bass will readily gobble an earthworm, whose home is far removed from the water . . .

I mention these things simply to encourage the reader to *experiment*. In fact, the user of artificial lures has no choice, when the fish persist in refusing his offerings. If one artificial fails to work, try an-other. Don't give up. For all you know, it could be a day when banana skins resemble small mullet . . .

Plugs fall into two main types: the floating and the sinking varie-

FLOATING PLUGS

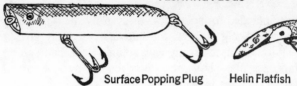

Surface Popping Plug

Helin Flatfish

Creek Chub Darter

Creek Chub Jointed Darter

Cisco Kid Topper

Topwater Mouse

SINKING PLUGS

Creek Chub Pikie

Norman Deep-Runner

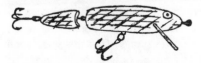

Norman Jointed Minnow

Phillips Midget Killer

SONIC PLUGS

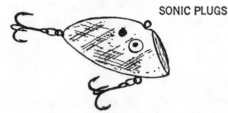

Norman Flasher

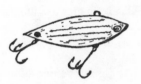

Garcia King Spot

Figure 4–1

ties. A tiny floater, intended for spinning—or even fly rod—use, may weigh only 1/16 ounce. A big plunker, for saltwater use, may go 3½ ounces, or more. Plugs are used mainly with spinning and bait casting rods, and the most popular sizes range between 1/8 and 5/8 of an ounce. (Several types of plugs are shown in *Figure 4–1*.)

A floating, or surface, plug may be pencil-thin, torpedo-shaped or blunt-headed—to name some of the most popular designs. The blunted head may be square, concave, etc. It permits the setting up of an attracting fuss when the lure is "popped" at the surface (i.e., when the rod tip is moved quickly). This plug may incorporate spinners fore and aft, also, to make noise. These small propellers set up flash, and vibrations, too, that attract fish.

A diving, or below-the-surface, plug may resemble the floating kind—as the illustration also shows—but it must either be weighted to sink gradually of its own accord, or it must employ a metal or plastic diving "lip" (plane) beneath the head. If the lure is of the self-sinking type, you need only slow down the retrieve to allow it to swim deeper, and vice versa. If the below-the-surface plug depends upon a mouthpiece for its operation, it will usually float when at rest, then dive under to start wiggling when line is retrieved. The stronger the retrieve, the greater the depth at which this plug will operate.

Another popular sinking type plug, one which depends upon built-in weight rather than a diving plane, is the so-called "sonic" variety. This one sets up a fish-attracting rattle as it vibrates in the water while being retrieved or trolled. The faster it is pulled through the water the greater the frequency of the vibrations that it will set up.

A well-manufactured plug will have a durable paint finish. And, especially if it is intended for saltwater use, the lure will make use of stainless steel hardware and (usually tinned) treble hooks that won't rust easily. There are customarily two gangs (clusters) of such hooks, although there may be three—or even only a single cluster. If the lure is to be used for large game fish which might pull the hooks free from their anchors, the barbs should be connected together, and to the lure eye. This is done by means of a strong piece of wire that is hidden from view, inside the lure body.

Jigs

The jig is but one of several effective metal lures in popular use today. Basically, it consists of a long-shanked single hook with a built-up lead head—this last to provide the required sinking and casting weight—and a body of feathers, real or artificial hair over the hook, as shown in *Figure 4–2*. Sometimes a few strips of tinsel (usu-

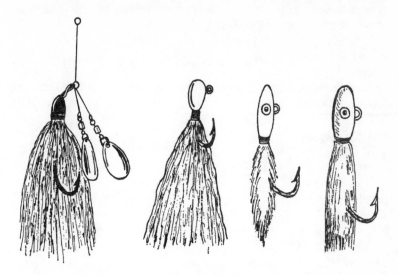

Figure 4–2   (Courtesy of Uncle Josh Bait Co.)

ally tarnish-resistant Mylar) are added to the body to provide fish-attracting flash. Plastic tails, instead of feathers or hair, have become popular for jigs in recent years, and such a lure is also shown in the illustration.

All jigs depend upon the angler to impart to them the necessary action to attract fish. This can be done by casting out the weighted lure and allowing it to sink to the depth where the fish are. A steady retrieve can then be started (i.e., a constant turning of the reel handles, at even speed). If this fails, the retrieve should be varied: by alternately moving the rod tip and reeling in two or three turns, for example—to cause the jig to dart and zoom and sink invitingly on its way in. A shrimp moves through the water in such erratic manner.

Should the quarry be feeding at the top, the retrieve should be begun at once, of course. And, if the fish are at or near the bottom, the jig should be allowed to sink to that position before beginning the retrieve. I've seen large ocean fish, amberjack and others, caught in this manner when other methods failed: a jig was allowed to sink straight down until it struck bottom, then brought straight up with a series of mighty, rod-bending jerks.

Bouncing a jig along the bottom—letting it alternately strike, then bounce upward again as you continue to reel in, or troll—can also prove effective in getting strikes.

Plastic Eels and Worms

A variation of the plastic-tailed jig is the artificial eel lure that uses this same soft material, as shown in *Figure 4–3*. This lure employs two

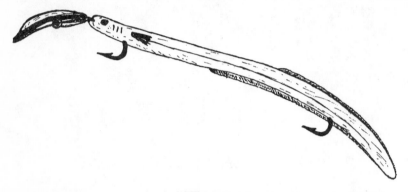

Figure 4–3

single hooks that are connected together inside the eel's long body. One is located near the front, the other in the tail area. Some eel lures employ a plastic skirt at the head, for added action and appeal. Others employ a tin squid, perhaps a spoon, at this position to give casting and trolling weight and better trolling action.

The undulating eel bait can be deadly. It was once used almost entirely for striped bass. But it has since been found capable of taking many other fish, including marlin.

A mini-version of the artificial eel is the popular plastic worm, or crawler, shown in *Figure 4–4*. These lifelike imitations come in

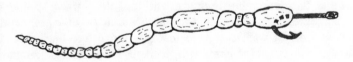

Figure 4–4

lengths from about three to six inches, and in a variety of colors. They not only feel like worms, but are molded closely to resemble worms—replete with segmented bodies that are tapered at head and tail. In fact, manufacturers go so far as to include a natural egg sac in the design of these lures. And some claim that they have even incorporated a tempting wormlike scent! ("Built-in flavor.")

Usually, a single barb is pierced through the head of the plastic worm, since it generally comes without its own barb. Some anglers, however, use up to three single hooks, especially if it be a long worm. These are connected by wire inside the body. Some worms, for ocean use, come in large sizes.

A plastic worm, retrieved *very* slowly along the bottom, can be deadly on big largemouth bass. A weedless hook makes the worm easier to fish where there are bottom growths and obstructions.

Multi-tube Trolling and Jigging Rigs

Another innovative plastic lure is the multi-tube device that initiates a small school of bait fish when it is jigged or trolled through the water, see *Figure 4–5*. For shallow trolling a conventional line may be

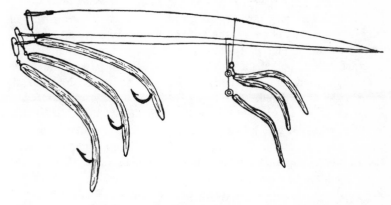

Figure 4–5

used with this device. For deep water fishing a weighted line is necessary, to prevent the somewhat cumbersome terminal rig from surfacing.

A jig, even a heavy spoon, with sufficient weight to sink the tubes to the bottom, is connected at the front end of the device for jigging.

The tubes, each only a few inches in length, may vary in number from three to half a dozen, or more. And the object—whether jigging or trolling—is to achieve that speed which will allow the flexible plastic tubes, each with its single built-in hook, to expand and contract in a manner that closely resembles a small school of swimming bait fish.

Metal Spoons and Spinners

Like the jig, metal spoons and spinners (see *Figure 4–6*) have long been used by anglers with great effectiveness. The spoon lure got its name from the eating utensil that it somewhat resembles. Spoons usually employ but a single hook, at the tail end, and are made with at least part of the body in bright finish (usually chromed) to provide flash. (Some spoons are painted on one side.)

These fishing lures wobble and dart when pulled through the water, beneath the surface, in a hook-upward position, thus resembling a crippled bait fish, or perhaps one that is having difficulty swimming in strong current, and hence at the mercy of larger fish. The depth at which the spoon will operate depends upon its weight (i.e., sink rate) and the speed at which it is pulled through the water.

A spinner lure may take various forms, as shown. To be worthy of the name spinner, however, the lure must employ a rounded, sometimes elongated, blade that is able to spin freely about a shank as the weighted lure is pulled through the water. Seldom is more than one such blade used, and it usually has a high polish finish, although some blades are painted.

A well-designed spinner lure will be made of rust-resistant materials. The blade will be well balanced, so that it will start to spin immediately, even with the slowest pull. To set up better the flashes and vibrations that attract fish, the blade is sometimes fluted.

To use a spinner lure you need only cast it out, let it sink to the desired depth, then begin a steady reel-in retrieve. The speed of the retrieve can be varied—at times even stopped briefly—should this prove necessary to provoke a fish into striking the lure.

Spinner lures come in weights from $\frac{1}{16}$ to about $\frac{1}{4}$ ounce, hence are ideal for light tackle casting use. Spoons, too, come in similar sizes—although some are considerably larger, and are used for trolling only, being too heavy for casting.

METAL SPOONS AND SPINNERS

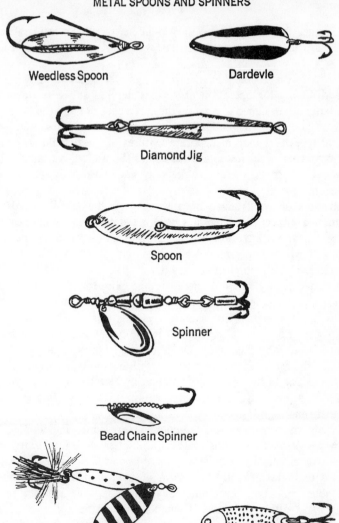

Weedless Spoon

Dardevle

Diamond Jig

Spoon

Spinner

Bead Chain Spinner

Garcia Abu-Reflex Spinner

Hopkins Stainless

Figure 4–6 (Courtesy of Uncle Josh Bait Co.)

Flies

Flies are the smallest, and most delicate, of all the artificial lures. There are three basic kinds of flies: wet, dry and bugs (see *Figure 4–7*).

Wet flies do, as the name implies, get wet. That is, they are intended mainly for operation at various depths, unlike the dry flies. The latter are designed to float on the surface, as are also the bugs.

Wet flies include the streamers, bucktails, nymphs and some special types that may incorporate features of the first three. Among the dry flies one finds the so-called bivisibles, variants, those "dressed" (adorned) with hackles only and those with various wing patterns.

(Dozens of books have been written on the subject of dry fly fishing—a subject that I feel has been made needlessly complicated— hence I have no intention of becoming technical on this type of fly fishing. I will summarize my advice simply by saying that this fine sport need not be complicated. Try it.)

In the category of bugs there are the poppers; the imitations of bugs, mice, frogs and other creatures that fish eat; and some special top water artificials. (For example, in this last classification would fall a special bug for taking sailfish in the ocean, a lure developed by pioneer ocean fly fisherman Dr. Webster Robinson, of Key West, Florida, the first man to take a sailfish with regulation fly tackle.)

Hook sizes for flies may vary from a tiny No. 22—for dry fly use— to a 4/0, or even larger, wet fly for tarpon. (Refer to Chapter 1 for a comparison of hook sizes.)

Briefly, the streamers and the bucktails are both wingless flies. The former is dressed with long feathers; the latter, with deer hair. These flies, like practically all the special types of wet flies, are not intended to imitate exactly any form of natural bait. They probably resemble small bait more than anything else. The nymph, on the other hand, although it, too, is wingless, should be a close replica of the pupa or larva of the particular kind of aquatic insect it is intended to imitate.

A bivisible is a dry fly tied, at the hook eye, with bristling hackles of contrasting colors. A variant resembles a winged spider. A hackle dry fly is wingless, dressed with hackles only. Other dry fly patterns may employ wings tied to the hook in an upright position, or at right angles to the shank, and so on.

WET FLIES (FRESH WATER)

Muddler Minnow
Streamer

Mickey Finn
Bucktail

HOB
Streamer

WET FLIES (SALT WATER)

Bonefish Streamer   Tarpon Streamer

Sailfish Streamer
(Yellow, with
Mylar tinsel strips)

NYMPHS

Green Damsel

Black Drake

Shrimp

TERRESTRIALS

Black Ant

Inch Worm

Cricket

DIVIDED WING DRY FLIES

Blue Dun

Quill Gordon

Royal Coachman

Figure 4–7

A popper is a bug with a blunt head—often concave—that permits this lure to cause a fish-attracting disturbance at the surface when line is retrieved with a sudden jerk. An actual bug—a so-called "bass bug," for example—can actually imitate any of several aquatic insects, and usually incorporates a hair body and wings. Hair is also used closely to imitate, both in size and color, mice, frogs, crawfish and other creatures that are either found naturally in the water, or that may drop in by accident. Bass bugs are also made with bodies of cork or balsa wood, and wings of feathers or hair.

Basically, a fly is simply a hook to which has been attached (i.e., held in position, usually by thread wrappings and cement) certain materials intended to make the lure resemble some object that a fish normally eats. It is a matter of historic record that men have been successfully fishing with flies since before the time of Christ. Should the reader fail to try this exciting mode of fishing, he is sadly limiting his enjoyment.

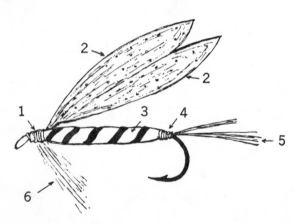

Figure 4–8 (1) Head, (2) Wings, (3) Body, (4) Butt, (5) Tail, (6) Hackle.

The ultimate thrill in fly fishing comes from catching a fish—a large one, especially—with a fly that you made yourself. So let's build such a lure right now, starting from the beginning. *Figure 4–8* designates the various parts of a fly.

First, we will select one of the proven patterns to copy—a streamer, since it is simple to make. I would urge the beginner not to experiment with fly design—not at the outset, at least. Stick to those designs that have proven to be fish catchers. That way you won't become discouraged.

Next, we will select a long-shanked, rust-resistant hook of good quality. For salt water use a stainless steel hook (the No. 254SS by Eagle Claw, for example) is preferred over the variety that may be plated with cadmium, nickel, etc. Let's settle for a 1/0, since such a size fly will catch a large trout, or a salmon.

We will now place the hook, with the barb downward, in a small hook vise, as shown in *Photo 9.* Such an inexpensive vise costs less than five dollars and is well worth the investment. A conventional bench vise can be used, but it will handicap your fly-tying movements.

Clamp the hook vise at the edge of a bench (the kitchen table will do).

You will need these additional items, all of which can be purchased for a total of ten dollars, or less: a thread bobbin, a small pair of sharp-nosed scissors, a bodkin needle, a pair of tweezers, a pair of hackle pliers, a spool of A-size nylon thread, a small bottle of cement (fingernail polish will do), some hair from the tail of a deer, squirrel or other animal, a few feathers from the neck of a rooster, miscellaneous short lengths of wool yarn and tinsel.

The bobbin holds the spool of thread, making it easier to handle, and we will use it to begin dressing our fly. Close-wrap a single foundation layer of the thread about the shank of the hook, without overlapping any of the turns. This thread base will better hold in position the dressing materials to be added later: the body and wings.

The initial thread layer is applied to the hook in this manner, as shown in *Photo 10:* using the thumb and forefinger of one hand, hold in position atop the hook shank—just behind the eye—a doubled-back-upon-itself length of thread, long enough to permit the free end to extend backward to the bend of the hook. Now, using the bobbin, start to wrap the thread back upon itself. After the first couple securing wraps have thus been made, pause long enough to shift the thumb and forefinger to the free end of the thread. Stretch this taut, atop the shank, and back toward the bend. Now complete the close-spaced wrapping about both stretched thread and hook shank.

When the wraps reach the point where the bend of the hook begins, stop wrapping. Hold the thread taut (to keep it from unwinding) and use the fingers of the other hand to slip a loop (half hitch) over the hook shank, starting from the eye end. Then, still keeping the thread taut, pull this anchoring knot tight at the point where the wrappings were stopped, as shown in *Photo 11*.

The original free end of the thread should be protruding slightly beyond the securing knot just made. Snip off this end, close to the knot, using the scissors. Do not, however, cut off the thread from the bobbin. Leave this hanging, as you will be using it again shortly. Meanwhile, apply a small amount of cement to secure the knot better, wiping off any excess.

Some fly tiers, saltwater flymen in particular, do not bother to install tails on their homemade flies. We shall install a tail, however, just to show you how it is done.

Select one of the rooster neck feathers. (You can purchase these hackles, should you prefer, dyed bright red, yellow, etc.) Pull off about a half dozen of the individual spines that make up this feather. Hold these together in a small bunch, with all the tips pointing in the same direction. Then cut the opposite ends off evenly, so all the little feathers will be of the same length.

Hold the bunched spines atop the hook shank, at the bend end, allowing the tips to extend about half an inch beyond the bend. Now use the bobbin to continue the thread wrapping (always in the same direction as the original wrap) to secure these small feather spines to the shank, as shown in *Photo 12*.

The extent of such wrapping will vary somewhat with the taste of the designer. Some fly tiers prefer a loose wrap here that doubles back over itself. Your aim should be to create a fly that is not too bulky, and hence not too heavy. When the tail has been secured to your satisfaction, make another half hitch at the point of the last wrap—which should have ended just behind the hook's eye—and leave the thread from the bobbin not cut, and hanging, for later use, as before. Once more, secure the dressing with a light coat of cement.

The body of the fly comes next. Various materials can be used here. Wool yarn, braided tinsel tubing, chenille, rayon floss are among the most popular. Let's use a short length of black wool for our fly body, overwrapped with silver tinsel (Mylar stripping) to provide the lure some fish-attracting flash.

We will secure the yarn and tinsel first. Do this by holding together, side by side, an end from each of the two materials. Place these ends over the last thread knot made. Then make several close thread wraps about both the ends, tying this off with the usual half hitch. Then continue to wind the thread, still in the same direction as the initial body winding, toward the head of the fly. (A slight spiral winding will prove satisfactory here.) Secure the thread, just behind the hook eye, with another hitch. This is done so the thread will be in position, later, to anchor both the body yarn and the tinsel strip there when these two materials reach that point. Now wind the yarn toward the eye, using tight turns. The tinsel ribbing is then wound, in turn, over the yarn in a spiral, to give a barber pole effect, as shown in *Photo 13*.

Secure both the yarn and the tinsel at the head of the fly, using several wraps of thread, tied off with a hitch. Snip off the excess body material, and turn to the fly's wings.

(*Note:* Should you prefer a fuller body than the one we have just completed, you can wrap the wool yarn—or other body material— back and forth upon itself several times, perhaps striving for a tapered body effect that will more closely resemble a small bait fish. The choice is yours; as are the colors used for tail, body and wings.)

To dress the fly's wings we will select four of the rooster feathers, each about two inches long. Strip away the shaft vanes, starting at the bottom, until only about a third of the original feather remains. Place these feather tips, with their shafts cut to appropriate length, and the ends even, atop the hook shank—just behind the eye. Wrap tightly with more thread, secure with the usual hitch, and trim away any excess, applying cement as the final step. (See *Photo 14*.)

We will use a hackle on our fly—since these "whiskers" at the head, that stand out at right angles to the shaft (i.e., so-called "Palmer-tied"), do improve a fly's effectiveness. Once more we will use a rooster neck feather.

Use the fingers to spread apart the spines on this feather, leaving them otherwise intact on the shaft, however. Then use thread to secure the lower end of the feather shaft to the hook shank, just behind the eye. Now, gripping the tip of the feather with the hackle pliers, wind the feather—on its edge—about the hook shank. Meanwhile, as you do this, use thread wrappings to secure the feather's now spread-apart spines to the shank, so these spines will stick up, to form a collar at the front end of the fly body. When the last of the feather has been wound about the shank, and used up thus, secure its tip to the shank with several more turns of thread, followed by the usual securing hitch. Trim and cement lightly. (Refer to *Photo 15*.)

We are now ready for the final step: completion of the head of the fly. Wrap tightly a dozen or so turns of thread between the hook eye and the hackle. The actual number of such turns will depend upon the number necessary to make a neat, tapered finish. To make such a finish a so-called "whip finish" is customarily employed. That is, the end of the thread is pulled taut in a manner that finds it buried under several of the wraps—held firmly there as the loops are pulled carefully tight. Sometimes a special, needlelike tool is used by fly tiers to probe beneath the turns, to snag the thread end and pull it through, for the final snubbing. When the whip finish has been completed, snip off the thread leading to the bobbin and apply a coat or two of cement.

When the cement has dried, you may wish to varnish the head. Perhaps you will want to paint an eye upon the head, to make the fly even more attractive (to you?).

Chances are that you've managed to fill the hook eye by this time with dried cement. So use a toothpick—some fly tiers prefer a bodkin, a needle-thin probe mounted inside a handle for holding—to clear any cement or varnish from the hook eye. Fail to do this, and you will not, of course, be able to fasten a leader tippet to the hook, later. A bodkin can also prove handy in positioning wings and hackles during the construction process.

By this stage you will appreciate that there can be many variations in wet and dry fly patterns. To a lesser extent, this also applies to bugs. You can make your own bugs with bodies of cork, balsa and styrofoam. Some anglers solve the body-shaping problem by making a bug from a carrot type, or other, float. This is done by using a portion of the float (usually it is cut into two pieces, leaving a top and bottom section, each of which can serve as the body of a bug). A tail may then be added, perhaps even hackles. Here again, however, let me urge you to copy proven patterns, designs that have proven capable of getting strikes.

In conclusion, I can think of few better ways to spend an otherwise long winter evening, than by making your own flies. Too, the materials you need will cost only about a tenth what the finished lure would cost if it were purchased. And nearly always the homemade fly lasts longer.

Chapter 5
A Brief Description of, and Where to Find, the Most Popular North American Game Fish

Despite careless deforestation, shameful pollution and a steadily increasing horde of more than fifty million anglers, the North American continent—the United States, particularly—offers sportsmen more kinds of fresh water game fish than any other country in the world. There are so many of these, in fact, that anglers become hopelessly confused.

And the situation is often nearly as bad in salt water.

This confusion is increased when fishermen persist in using local names that are often misleading. (Anglers shun the hard-to-pronounce names used by scientists, who accurately classify the various species on the basis of scale count, fin structure, etc.)

As a result, we find one of the perches mistakenly called a "walleyed pike"—while a white bass is referred to in Midwest fresh waters as a "striper," a title reserved on both coasts for a much larger, ocean fish that ventures inland mainly to spawn.

This chapter is intended to help both the beginner and the experienced angler to identify what he has caught. By referring to the description associated with each of the following fish, no longer need an ordinary whitefish be hopefully considered a prize brook trout, and so on. As an additional aid, and to encourage further research where it may be needed, the scientific name is also given in each case.

What follows should also give the reader a good idea where to go in North America to find game fish of his choice. The largemouth black bass of the American Southeast, for instance, remains second to none in size—and will never be found swimming in salt water alongside a black sea bass. The dainty golden trout of the High Sierra, perhaps the most beautiful of all fish, does not venture into lowland lakes where roams the fierce muskellunge. The catfish are associated with quiet, muddy waters—yet the sportiest of the clan, the channel cat, prefers swift, clear streams.

The reader planning to fish outside his own immediate area will be prudent to communicate beforehand, if possible, with that region to learn what to bring, when is the best time to fish, etc. Additional information can be gotten upon arrival, for fishing conditions change constantly; in the coastal areas, particularly. Later chapters will describe the best tackle and methods to catch the various fish.

FRESH WATER PANFISH

The Sunfishes

The members of this large and tasty clan are often described by the general term "panfishes," since their small size permits them to be placed whole in a pan for cooking. These spunky little fish seldom weigh over two pounds and may go only half that size. But they are easy to find and easy to catch, being not nearly so elusive as many of the other species.

Look for sunfish in quiet waters throughout the United States: in small coves and shallows of power reservoirs; in ponds and streams; under boats (including, very likely, the skiff from which you may be fishing!); close alongside dock pilings and boathouses; hard up against rocks and submerged logs; in fact, in any reasonably clean water that offers food and protective bottom growths.

Several dozen species of sunfishes swim in U.S. waters, all of them looking much the same in body profile, but not coloration. The largest single family of these sunfishes may be the *Lepomis,* to which belongs the **bluegill** (*L. macrochirus*), considered by many loyal followers to be the scrappiest of all the panfish. To hear one of these little fellows surface and smack your bait or lure with characteristic kissing sound is a sure indication of brisk cane pole and bobber (or other light tackle) action to follow. These bream are particularly active while "bedding" (spawning), at which time you can often locate such hot spots by the odor given off by the fish.

The **redbreast sunfish** (*L. auritus*), the **pumpkinseed** (*L. gibbosus*), the **spotted** (*L. punctatus*), **green** (*L. cyanellus*), **redear** (*L. microlophus*) and **longear** (*L. megalotis*) sunfishes are also favorite American panfishes of the *Lepomis* family. The spotted (*punctatus*) or "stumpknocker," gets its unusual name from its habit of striking noisily against stumps and roots to snap up insects that crawl down to the water line.

Some other sunfishes that are regularly pursued by anglers are **black crappie** (*Pomoxis nigromaculatus*) and the **white crappie** (*P. annularis*); the **rock bass** (*Ambloplites rupestris*); the **warmouth** (*Chaenobryttus coronarius*); and a little green fish called the **flier** (*Centrarchus macropterus*).

The Perches

There are over twenty species of these, some of them being sunfish, and I shall list here only those most commonly fished for and caught.

It has been said that American boys learn to fish first for the popular and widespread **yellow perch** (*Perca flavescens*). This one- to two-pound fish (the record is slightly over four) is found from Nova Scotia to the Carolinas; from western Pennsylvania to Kansas; and in scattered introduced sites on the Pacific slope. Look for this tasty little fellow in quiet ponds and streams, around grass beds (where they feed upon minnows) and pilings, in deeper water over gravel or rock bottom.

The **walleye,** or pike, perch (*Stizostedion vitreum*) is probably the most sought-after of the perches. It seldom exceeds six or eight pounds, although the record is twenty-five, and is found in lakes (mainly), being common in the Great Lakes region. This fish ranges throughout Canada and from Nebraska south to Alabama and Georgia.

The **sauger,** or sand, pike (*S. canadense*) is a one- to two-pound fish of the Great Lakes, east-central Canada, and the upper reaches of the Ohio, Mississippi and Missouri rivers. Look for it in big lakes and silted rivers.

The so-called **Sacramento perch** (*Archoplites interruptus*) is a small sunfish (seldom more than a foot long) found in limited numbers in California, in the drainage of the San Joaquin and Sacramento rivers. It carries a spot on the gill cover.

The Basses

The scientists will tell you that the fresh water fish which American anglers commonly refer to as basses—that is, the largemouth, smallmouth, spotted and redeye—are actually sunfishes, whereas the true members of the bass family are the white and yellow bass and the white perch (!). It seems wise, however, for the purpose of this book, to list them all here in one place, as follows:

The **largemouth black bass** (*Micropterus salmoides*) is the single fresh water game fish most often pursued by U.S. anglers. It is found mainly from southern Canada southward through the Mississippi drainage and eastern United States to Florida (where it grows largest) and parts of northeastern Mexico. There is also good bigmouth fishing, however, in the northwestern United States (where it was introduced in the 1800s) and California and elsewhere.

Both this fine game fish and its two close relatives, the **smallmouth black bass** (*M. dolomieui*) and the **spotted,** or Kentucky, bass (*M. punctulatus*) like to hide in weed beds, behind sunken logs, etc., and dart from such cover to seize minnows and other passing prey. The largemouth and spotted species usually prefer warm, sluggish—even still—waters, often with muddy bottoms—whereas the smallmouth likes swift, clear streams with rocky shores and bottoms; also, pools below dams, and deep lake gravel bars. When the bigmouth is not hiding in dense grass (cast *close* against such cover, sometimes even inside it—more on this in later chapters) look for him near shoreline points and over "drop-offs," bars that slope quickly into deeper water.

Bigmouth bass average two to five pounds, a fifteen-pounder being a rare Florida catch; smallmouths and Kentucky bass average perhaps a pound to three pounds, a five-pounder being an outstanding catch, in either case.

The smallmouth has been widely introduced and is found from California and British Columbia in scattered locations to the U. S. East Coast, and in the Great Lakes, Mississippi, Ohio and Tennessee river systems. The spotted bass is common in the Gulf states and roams northward about to a line between Kansas and West Virginia.

The **redeye bass** (*M. coosae*) is a small bass with range limited to streams and rivers of Georgia and Alabama. A pound or two is the average weight.

White bass (*Morone chrysops*) are found from south-central Canada eastward throughout the Great Lakes-St. Lawrence area and New York State and southward through the Mississippi Valley to Arkansas and Texas. This fresh water species of a saltwater family (it can be easily confused, in the same size, with the striped bass, a saltwater fish) averages from one to three pounds. A school fish, it can be easily frightened (put down) when encountered feeding at the surface of deep, still lakes—although it also frequents streams and rivers.

The **yellow bass** (*M. interrupta*) runs about the same size, but prefers the southern portion of the Mississippi drainage, although it is found as far north as Minnesota, too.

The **white perch** (*M. americana*), sometimes called sea perch, is a bass that is at home in either fresh or salt water. It is found in the eastern United States, from Canada to the Carolinas, in sizes seldom over three pounds. Sometimes it becomes landlocked in fresh water.

The Trouts

There are two main families of fresh water trouts: (1) the true trouts, easily distinguished by their body spots that are *darker* than the background color; and (2) the chars, which have spots that are *lighter* than the rest of the body.

The first group includes the **rainbow trout** (*Salmo gairdneri*), which becomes known as a steelhead, should it migrate to salt water, and a subspecies of the rainbow, called the Kamloops trout, a usually much larger fish that is usually found in deep lakes; the **cutthroat trout** (*S. clarki*), which is also known as a "coaster," should it swim to the sea; the **brown trout** (*S. trutta*); and the **golden** (*S. aguabonita*).

In the second family, the chars, one finds the **Dolly Varden** (*Salvelinus malma spectabilis*); the **lake trout,** or Mackinaw (*S. namaycush*); the **Eastern brook trout** (*S. fontinalis*); and several other, less popular, species of chars.

The rainbow is considered by many anglers to be the prize catch among the fresh water trouts—perhaps because of its fight and vivid colors—although there are others that battle quite as well, I've found. This fish, like the cutthroat and golden trout, is a native of the Far West, yet it has been successfully transplanted elsewhere throughout the United States, where water has had abundant oxygen and did not exceed 75 degrees. Basically, however, the rainbow remains native to waters of the Rockies and the Pacific slope, from Mexico to Alaska.

Rainbows like to frequent active, well-aerated streams above falls, particularly along the edges of white water, and both low and high altitude lakes, especially the latter. Big rainbows will lie deep in lake bottom holes. Late evening and early morning are usually the best times to take this beautiful fish.

The cutthroat is said to be the ancestor from which all the other pioneer western trout sprang. Being a true Westerner, it has successfully resisted artificial stocking elsewhere, and is still found mainly west of the Rocky Mountains, from northern California to southeastern Alaska.

The cutthroat gets its odd name from a red splash of color under its lower jaw, an identifying mark that remains until—and if—it migrates to salt water. Should it do this, look for the cutthroat trout to feed upon young steelhead and salmon in quiet tidal rivers, especially where small streams empty into shoals of such waterways; also, over gradually deepening gravel bottoms and around kelp and other grass beds. On the other hand, should the cutthroat decide to remain at home, this will usually be some high lake or swift, splashing stream, at least a couple thousand feet above sea level.

The brown trout is not a native American. It was brought to this country from England—where it had long been famous—about the mid-1880s. This wise game fish has since been widely and successfully planted in sluggish rivers and warm lakes of the United States, and parts of Canada. It and the brook trout (actually one of the chars) are the only trouts that most Easterners ever see, although the once abundant brookie has largely disappeared, thanks to man's continuing deforesting of the land.

The golden, the fourth of the true American trouts, is aptly named. There is no mistaking this golden-bellied fish once you catch one. But you will have to go west, usually to the High Sierra range, to do so. And I mean high, to clear streams and lakes. The successful angler must exercise himself to catch this gleaming fish.

Dolly Varden is a dainty name for a scavenger trout that likes to destroy the young of other game fish when it is not prowling the bottom for refuse, like a shark. Hence, this colorfully spotted char is held in low regard by many anglers, who seem to forget that all trouts are cannibals. I've caught Dollies from Montana to Alaska, their normal range, and have found these bull trout to run not only consistently larger, but often scrappier, than rainbows and some of the other favorites. Look for Dolly Varden in streams, rivers and lakes (sometimes landlocked) wherever there is abundant natural food.

The lake trout (also called Mackinaw and togue) is the real big boy of the trout family, the rod and reel record being sixty-three pounds. (Most other trouts average from a half to perhaps three pounds, although the records for rainbow, cutthroat, brown, Eastern brook and golden trout are, respectively: 37, 41, 39½, 14½ and 11 pounds. These records were established many years ago.)

The lake trout is usually caught by trolling deep—often sixty feet or more—in large, quiet lakes, for this pale but powerful char prefers water that remains 40 and 50 degrees the year around. In spring, shortly after ice-out, lakers will move into shallows to feed; and again, in fall, to spawn. These fish are found from the Great Lakes north, and west, to Alaska. Lake trout are so plentiful in the Yukon I recently saw homemade signs along the Alaska Highway offering freshly caught lakers for sale; they are good eating.

The Eastern brook trout, a delight to catch and to eat, is still found from northeastern United States up into eastern Canada. Ideally suited for rearing in hatcheries, the square-tailed brookie has been successfully introduced elsewhere on this continent, notably from California northward through British Columbia. This fish likes well-aerated, clear and cold (seldom above 50 degrees) spring-fed pools and brooks, spawning upstream in the latter, or in the shallower portions of lakes.

The Salmons

These game and food fishes of the genera *Salmo* and *Oncorhynchus* are pink-fleshed, and of the same family as the true trouts. Salmon habitually swim from salt to fresh water to spawn, after which act practically all the half dozen Pacific Coast species of North American salmon die. The two eastern species, the Atlantic and the landlocked, seldom die from spawning.

The biggest of the West Coast fish is the **king,** or **chinook salmon** (*Oncorhynchus tshawytscha*). These powerful fish have been taken to 126 pounds (in Alaska), the rod and reel record being a ninety-two-pound chinook fought in British Columbia in 1959. Most, however, run ten to thirty pounds. Kings are found in sea-connecting coastal bays and rivers from southern California to Alaska.

The next most important of the western salmons is the **silver,** or **coho** (*O. kisutch*). This one averages considerably less than the king, a record fish being one in the twenty-pound class, in local competitions. This is a very exciting game fish, however, particularly when taken with flies, which it accepts quite readily. In addition to their normal Pacific range (similar to the king's), silvers are now also caught in the Great Lakes area, thanks to a successful Michigan stocking program that began to pay off handsomely with cohos weighing up to twenty pounds, sometimes even more, in 1967—although this amazing sport has since abated somewhat.

Four other Pacific species of salmons—the **sockeye,** or red (*O. nerka*), the **humpback,** or pink (*O. gorbuscha*), the **dog,** or chum (*O. keta*), and the **kokanee** (*O. nerka kennerlyi*)—vary in size from about one half pound to twelve pounds. These smaller fish often do not strike as readily as the others, hence are less pursued by sportsmen.

The most glamorous of the eastern species—and the fish that many enthusiastic followers consider to be the most sporting of all the salmon—is the **Atlantic** (*Salmo salar*). This fish has made world-famous the waters of eastern Canada: coastal rivers like the Resti-gouche and Matapédia, for example. This gleaming silver flash swims mainly northward from Cape Cod to Iceland, in yard-long sizes, usually from ten to twenty pounds, but can go much higher.

The second salmon found in the eastern United States is the **landlocked** (*S. salar sebago*). This non-seagoing relative of the Atlantic is golden-brown, instead of silver, is smaller (five pounds, or less, as a rule) and is found in lakes (where smelts are available for food) from Maine to Labrador.

Salmon spawn from spring to December (the Atlantic salmon, in fall) and sometimes you can hear the great silver horde moving resolutely inland to do this, even before you catch sight of the advancing, splashing, surging fish. The beautiful, doomed fish yield to an overpowering compulsion to return to the water of their birth. They leap incredibly high to get past roaring waterfalls and other obstructions. They wriggle through seemingly impossible shallows, often cutting and tearing their magnificent bodies mercilessly in the process. Their uncanny homing instinct is said to be 97 per cent effective.

In Alaska I've watched big brown bears wade hungrily into fish-choked streams deftly to scoop out big salmon onto the bank, to be consumed alive. Beyond that, however, it seems such a huge waste as the fish complete the spawning act and proceed to die. They lie in the water like cordwood as unused stomachs continue to shrivel up and body colors change to telltale scarlet, the grim sign that once healthy tissue is steadily decaying. A sobering sight, indeed.

After about one year spent in the fresh water of their parents' birth, the young salmon invariably swim back to the sea, there to spend most of their lives in the estuarine and deeper waters—in preparation for the fatal return inland.

The Pikes

These long and slim members of the *Esox* family are mean, unpredictable fish. This is especially true of the **northern pike** (*E. lucius*), a predator that seems to delight in killing every smaller living thing within striking range as it swims Nebraska-Missouri-New York northward through the Great Lakes region, Canada and Alaska. The record northern is a forty-six-pounder (but is another of those records established over thirty years ago; conditions have changed much since then!). Most of these lean fish with the out-jutting lower jaw weigh from one to ten pounds as they frequent cold and clear, weedy lake shallows and sluggish streams, often with rocky areas.

A close look-alike, but a bigger fish, is the **muskellunge** (*E. masquinongy*). The evil-eyed musky is a moody loner, found in similar waters from the Great Lakes and upper Mississippi drainages northward into Canada. Two subspecies have a more limited range: the **northern,** or tiger, muskellunge (*E. masquinongy immaculatus*) swims in lakes in Minnesota and Wisconsin, and the **chautauqua** musky (*E. masquinongy ohiensis*) is found in scattered lakes from the Ohio River system to the St. Lawrence River. Muskies grow to as much as seventy pounds, but average only about five to fifteen. They are edible, like the pike and pickerels.

The pickerels are the smallest of the pikes. There are three kinds, the largest being the Eastern, or **chain pickerel** (*E. niger*), a two- or three-pound fish (the record is nine and a half) that is found east of the Allegheny Mountains, from New England to Florida, and west to Texas. The two smaller pickerels, the **grass,** or mud (*E. vermiculatus*), and the barred, or **redfin** (*E. americanus*), are found in substantially this same range and seldom exceed a pound in weight.

The Catfishes

There are more than a dozen kinds of these, all easily recognized by the eight "whiskers" or barbels that grow from the jaws. The largest member of this family is the **blue** (*Ictalurus furcatus*) catfish that swims southward through the Ohio drainage to the Gulf of Mexico, and westward to Kansas and Minnesota. The biggest blue taken so far with rod and reel is a ninety-seven-pounder, but most go under twenty. Like nearly all its relatives, the blue prefers mud-bottomed streams and lakes.

The **channel catfish** (*I. punctatus*) is an exception, however. It likes clear, fast streams as it ranges from south-central Canada west to Montana, east to the St. Lawrence, and south through the Mississippi drainage to the Gulf states, in about five-pound average size (the 1964 record is fifty-eight pounds; a South Carolina fish).

Scattered throughout the United States are three additional catfish that are called "bullheads": the **yellow** (*I. natalis*); the **brown** (*I. nebulosus*); and the **black bullhead** (*I. melas*). The last two are also found in parts of southern Canada. All are small fish (a pound or two, though the brown may go twice that) found in weedy ponds and sluggish, muddy streams and rivers.

The **white catfish** (*I. catus*) is a scavenger, like the others, frequenting the same kind of waters, from New Jersey to Texas to California (where it was introduced) in sizes of a pound or two.

The **flathead catfish** (*Pylodictis olivaris*), also called the mud cat, is a big fellow found in the large, sluggish rivers that flow from both sides into the Mississippi drainage, the lower half in particular. These catfish exceed 100 pounds, with twenty-five to fifty common.

Grayling, Sheefish and Arctic Char

Related to the trouts and salmons, the grayling is a tasty, yet not very scrappy, little fish (usually from one to two pounds) that prefers clear and cold shallow streams, preferably gravel-bottomed, and (some) lakes. It can be readily identified by its swept-back, seemingly ridiculously high and long dorsal fin that often breaks water as it feeds. Two kinds of grayling swim in North American waters, and their names indicate the approximate distribution: the **Arctic,** or Alaska, **grayling** (*Thymallus arcticus*) and the **Montana,** sometimes called Michigan, **grayling** (*T. tricolor*).

The Arctic species is also found in Canada, in the far north-western portion, especially.

The **sheefish,** or inconnu (*Stenodus leucichthys*), grows to at least fifty pounds and is limited to the Arctic Circle region of Alaska, where they strike cast spoons, like the Dardevle. The Kotzebue Sound and Kobuk River waters of this region are particulary good. There the shee has been taken from thirteen to twenty-two pounds. Perhaps the best place for these close relatives of the Dolly Varden trout, however, is in Lake Aleknagik, at the mouth of the Agulowak River. Sheefish are good eating.

Some Other Fresh Water Fishes

The **common,** or American, **shad** (*Alosa sapidissima*) is found throughout the length of both the Atlantic and Pacific coasts, where it migrates in season into sea-connecting rivers to spawn. At that time, both males and females will strike lures and flies (use a sinking line for the latter). These two- to six-pound game fish grow to twice that size on the East Coast, even larger in the Pacific (where they range as far north as Alaska). This shad is the largest of the herring family.

I shall include three other members of the salmon and trout family that are fished for, but are not particularly good fighters: the lake herring, or **cisco** (*Coregonus artedi*); the **lake whitefish** (*C. clupea-formis*); and the **Rocky Mountain whitefish** (*C. williamsoni*). The first two swim in lakes in Canada and the Great Lakes-New York area; I've caught the third in Montana mountain streams.

The **mooneye** (*Hiodon tergisus*), sometimes called white shad, is a small school fish (one pound, or less) of the Mississippi and Great Lakes to Manitoba areas. It has a very large eye.

The **fresh water drum** (*Aplodinotus grunniens*) is a croaker, and may make the same protesting sound as its saltwater namesakes when caught, although it grows considerably larger than they (i.e., to sixty pounds, which ranks it with the biggest of fresh water fish). This drum is found over muddy bottoms from the Manitoba-Ontario-Great Lakes area south to the Gulf states.

The Fresh Water Rough Fishes

The **carp** (*Cyprinus carpio*) is an Asian food fish that was foolishly introduced to the United States. It has since spread throughout the country, the central and western areas, in particular, where it destroys more desirable fish and their habitat. It prefers quiet, muddy water and grows to twenty-five pounds and upward (record is fifty-five).

The **northern redhorse** (*Moxostoma aureolum*) is a member of the sucker family, as is the **white sucker** (*Catostomus commersonii*). These toothless bottom-feeders are found roughly in the eastern halves of (southern) Canada and the United States clear down to the Gulf for the white sucker, in sizes one to ten pounds.

The **burbot** (*Lota lota*) is a fresh water member of the cod family. It comes in sizes up to about twenty pounds (about five is average) in large lakes (when not spawning in rivers) from New England to the Great Lakes states, and from eastern Canada to Alaska (a subspecies in the last case).

The **paddlefish,** or spoonbill (*Polyodon spathula*), of muddy Mississippi Valley waters has been caught in sizes over 150 pounds. This duckbill resembles somewhat the sawfish of salt water.

The **hackleback sturgeon** (*Scaphirhynchus platorynchus*) is but one member of the Northern Hemisphere fresh and saltwater fishes that are throwbacks from primitive times. They sometimes come in very large sizes, and the roe is the source of the delicacy caviar.

The **alligator gar** (*Lepisosteus spatula*) can also grow very large, and is also a carry-over from prehistoric times. There are four species of these fresh water wolves found in the eastern United States (mainly) from Great Lakes to Gulf—the longnose, shortnose, spotted and alligator, the last of which may reach six feet. They are members of the ganoid family, as are also the sturgeon, paddlefish and bowfin.

The **bowfin,** or mudfish (*Amia calva*), of central and eastern North America, frequents weedy, muddy lakes and rivers (swamps). It comes in sizes to about twelve pounds; a vicious predator and strong fighter.

POPULAR SALTWATER BOTTOM FISHES

It will be impossible to include here the many different species that are apt to grab one's hook in the salt. In the rocky shallows, kelp beds and bays of the California coast alone there are dozens of different sculpins, greenlings, surf and so-called "rock fishes" (over fifty varieties of these last).

1. Big game and regular (lighter) boat rods, spinning, fly and bait casting rods, shown left to right. (Courtesy of Garcia Corp.)

2. A bait casting reel.
(Courtesy of Garcia Corp.)

3. A spinning reel.

4. Another kind of spinning reel, sometimes called a spin-cast reel.

5. Three kinds of fly reels. Notice that the automatic reel on the left has no handle.

6. A trolling reel used for larger fish.

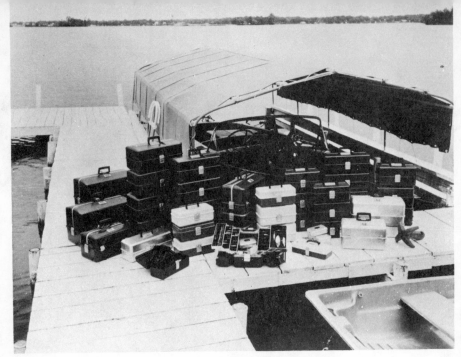

7. A variety of tackle boxes made by UMCO.

8. A professional party boat guide casts a giant net into a school of mullet in pursuit of bait for his tarpon fishing customers.

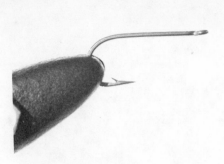

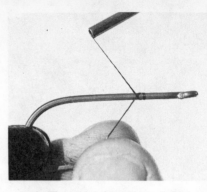

9. This and the following six pictures show how expert Miami, Florida, fly-tier Lefty Kreh dresses a fly. Here he places the hook with the barb downward in a small hook vise.

10. The initial thread layer being applied to the hook.

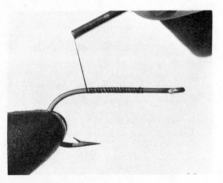

11. Keeping the thread taut the anchoring knot is pulled tight at the point where the wrappings were stopped.

12. The small feather spines are secured to the shank by continuing to thread the wrapping with a bobbin (always in the same direction as the original wrap).

13. The tinsel ribbing being wound over the yarn in a spiral.

14. The rooster feathers, used for dressing the fly's wings, are wrapped tightly with thread to secure the hitch and the excess is trimmed away. A coat of cement is applied as the final step.

15. The final trimming done, a final coat of cement is lightly applied.

16. The finished fly.

17. A discouraging sight for the fisherman, a dock stacked up with anglers.

Saltwater Panfish

The ever pleasing **spot,** or **salt water bream** (*Lagodon rhomboides*), deserves a prominent place in this grouping. This delicious five- to ten-inch (less than a pound) young anglers' delight gets its name from the pea-size black shoulder spot, worn adjacent to the gill cover. This scrappy little pinfish swims in schools from Massachusetts to Texas. Look for it in inlets and shallow bays; in the vicinity of bottom growth, rocks, docks, etc.

The **porgy,** a somewhat larger panfish of the *Stenotomus* and *Calamus* families (there are at least six different kinds of porgies), is found over substantially this same range, and the West Indies, depending upon the species involved, particularly around rocks and reefs. The **scup,** or northern porgy, is found in schools mainly off Cape Cod.

The red-mouthed **grunts** of the *Haemulon* family come in even greater variety. These little warm water fish average less than a pound, and often emit audible grunts of protest when caught from Panama north to the Florida Keys and Gulf Coast (the white grunt, somewhat larger, ranges on northward to Cape Hatteras). Grunts feed mainly at night, around reefs, over both rock and sand bottoms.

The **snapper** family (*Lutjanus*) is found (mostly in schools) from Panama north to Texas and Florida, on the Atlantic side, and in the Pacific as far north as Mexico, depending upon species. The wily **mangrove,** or gray, **snapper** frequents tidal mangrove areas in sizes to four pounds and is probably the wisest of the lot; the brown trout of the sea (*L. griseus*). Somewhat larger is the **red snapper,** or muttonfish (*L. analis*), which can go to twenty-five pounds. The **yellowtail snapper** (*Ocyurus chrysurus*) and the **dog snapper** (*Lutjanus jocu*) each average but a couple pounds, or less. The dog, however, grows to sizes said to exceed 100 pounds in the Caribbean—hardly a panfish.

I recall the time that one of these huge **pargo** swam leisurely beneath our skiff as a guide and I fished with light tackle over the world's second largest barrier reef, off the coast of British Columbia. I tried frantically to catch this dog snapper, estimated to weigh seventy-five pounds, but could not entice the big fellow to strike.

Look for snapper over inshore and offshore reefs, and around wharfs, bridge pilings, other obstructions in the water.

The **opaleye** (*Girella nigricans*) is a Pacific fish that averages around two pounds (spinning record is five and a half) and swims from about mid-California southward. It has large, opalescent blue eyes, frequents rocky shores and can provide fine fly rod sport at times.

The **barred surf perch** (*Amphistichus argenteus*) of central and southern California beaches is another little fish that is particularly popular with young fishermen. Averages less than a pound.

A **whiting**, or northern kingfish (*Menticirrhus saxatilis*), can be easily recognized by its catfishlike lower jar barbel as it swims over sandy coastal bottoms from Maine to Chesapeake Bay in one- to five-pound sizes, some going on to Florida. A southern kingfish (*M. americanus*) is found in the surf, also, from the Chesapeake to Texas, as is the small (to eighteen inches) Gulf kingfish (*M. littoralis*).

The **corbina**, or corvina (*M. undulatus*), is a Pacific Coast member of this family. It is found in the surf, over sandy bottoms, in sizes one to about four pounds from about San Francisco to the Gulf of California.

The **common croaker** (*Micropogon undulatus*) averages a pound or two and frequents coastal shallows, often grassy estuaries, in small groups from Cape Cod southward throughout the Gulf of Mexico. It may give forth a croaking sound, being a member of the large and complex drum family of fishes that can use their swim bladders to make audible noises.

Several West Coast croakers swim through inshore waters from San Francisco southward and range from one to six pounds: the **yellowfin croaker** (*Umbrina roncador*); the **spotfin** (*Roncador stearnsi*); the **black croaker** (*Sciaena saturna*); and the **California kingfish** (*Genyonemus lineatus*).

The sea, or **black drum** (*Pogonias cromis*) is the only member of the drummers that shall be mentioned here, since it is the most common of this sluggish, bottom-hugging and hardly sporting clan. It swims in schools from New York to Texas, frequenting the surf, inlets and bays, in sizes three to six pounds (but sometimes over 100, too!) as it feeds slowly, mainly upon shrimps and shellfish.

The edible **cabezone** (*Scorpaenichthys marmoratus*) is one of the most popular of the West Coast scaleless, shallow water sculpins. This gaudy yet heavy-lidded and ugly fish swims from British Columbia to southern California, in two- to ten-pound sizes (but can go to twenty).

Larger Saltwater Fish

The widely distributed **jacks** (genus *Caranx*) are often shunned by sport fishermen, probably since these fish are not commonly eaten (save by the poor, usually in chowders). Yet these powerful bulldogs of the salt—which resemble permit and pompano, but are not related —have spared many a guide embarrassment when more desirable game fish refused to strike.

I have taken big **horse-eye** (*Caranx sexfasciatus*) and **crevalle** (*C. hippos*) jacks in the Bahamas and lower Caribbean that punished my light tackle—and me—more than could nearly any other fish the same size. Each of these two fish may vary in size from one to thirty pounds, or more. The horse-eye ranges northward from Panama as far as Virginia, in small schools like the other, and habitually in or near the Gulf Stream. The crevalle is often a loner, continuing farther north to Cape Cod, both offshore and inshore. It likes to enter inlets and swim beneath bridges and around docks.

A Pacific subspecies of the crevalle roams from Panama to the Gulf of California. A smaller jack (one to five pounds), the **blue runner** (*C. crysos*), has a black spot on its gill and swims from the Caribbean to Canada in schools, averaging less than two pounds.

The biggest and sportiest of all the jacks, the **amberjack** (*Seriola lalandi*), may weigh over 100 pounds (fifteen to twenty is average). This tackle-smasher abounds in tropic waters, where it prefers offshore reefs, swimming alone or in small groups. In the Atlantic it likes Florida, although it also roams north to Massachusetts. A Pacific version (*S. colburni*) swims in Mexican and Lower California waters.

Pollock (*Pollachius virens*), sometimes called Boston bluefish, or green cod, is not a member of either family. This cold water school fish may weigh four pounds, or ten times that, as it swims offshore from Virginia to Nova Scotia.

The Atlantic **tomcod** (*Microgadus tomcod*) and its Pacific relative (*M. proximus*) has a barbel hanging from its lower jaw and ranges from Virginia to Newfoundland, and mid-California to Alaska. These are small fish, seldom over a pound in size.

The **Atlantic cod** (*Gadus callarias*) is a seven- to twelve-pound fish caught with bait on the bottom, and in the surf and around inshore rocks, from Virginia (mainly New York) to eastern Canada. The tackle record is a seventy-four-pound Maine fish, taken in 1960.

The tasty blackfish, or **tautog** (*Tautoga onitis*), likes to haunt wrecks and rocky bottoms, in depths around thirty-five feet, from the Carolinas to the Canadian border. It averages two to ten pounds.

The **sheepshead** (*Archosargus probatocephalus*) has a head profile that resembles a sheep's—if you can stretch your imagination a bit. This bottom-feeding, Nova Scotia to Texas fish, seeks mollusks in wrecks, over shell reefs, about pilings, etc. It averages two to six pounds and can be easily recognized by its seven (usually) black, vertical color bands about the silver-green body. There is also a **California sheepshead** (*Pimelometopon pulcher*), with canine teeth, and much more colorful (as are many West Coast fish) in rose and black. It goes five to fifteen pounds and is found from the Santa Barbara area south to Mexico's Gulf of California.

The **flounder,** or fluke, belongs to the more than 500 species of flatfishes (of *Paralichthys* and other genera) that include also the halibut, turbots and soles. It is one of the strangest fish in the sea. A young flounder has body coloration on both sides, and eyes that are normally placed. With growth, however, its body changes to permit a one-sided adult life. The underside becomes white, and the second eye actually moves up onto the upper side of the head, to settle there permanently, close beside the first!

The familiar mottled **brown fluke** of the Atlantic seaboard (*Paralichthys dentatus*) weighs from one to twelve pounds. The likewise flat as a dish and huge **California halibut** (*P. californicus*) may weigh sixty pounds. And an even larger halibut, one weighing 300 and 400 pounds and upward (to 700), and as much as four feet in width, frequents deep waters off both coasts: from San Francisco to Alaska and from New Jersey to Greenland.

The **tripletail** (*Lobotes surinamensis*) is a hard-striking edible game fish of about seven to thirty pounds that swims in the Caribbean and Gulf of Mexico (some going on to Cape Cod). Nicknamed "sleeping fish" for its habit of resting—seeking shade and protection—beneath buoys, logs and other floating debris, I've caught them on artificial lures off the mouth of the Mississippi River while doing this.

The tastiest fish that I've found in salt water are the **common pompano** (*Trachinotus carolinus*) and the **round pompano** (*T. falcatus*), the former particularly. These one- to three-pound ocean fish travel in small schools along coastal beaches, and in inlets and estuaries from the Carolinas southward throughout the Gulf of Mexico and Caribbean.

ere are several other members of the pompano family, including
less than a pound (usually) **gaff-topsail pompano** (*T. palometa*)
f the West Indies, Florida and Bermuda—and the powerful permit,
to be discussed later.

The **cobia,** or crab-eater (*Rachycentron canadus*), is a fine game
fish with small head and olive-colored back that ranges from Panama
to Jamaica, Gulf of Mexico (abundant off Mississippi), the Bahamas,
Virginia and Massachusetts. It comes in ten to twenty pounds, usually,
has been taken over 100 (in 1938) with recent record tackle catches
over sixty-four (in 1965). Cobia frequent coastal bays, often in the
vicinity of buoys and other navigational aids. Common in Chesapeake
Bay area.

There are two main kinds of **sea trout:** the **spotted** (*Cynoscion
nebulosus*) and the spotless, or **gray** (*C. regalis*). The spotted averages
somewhat less than the three- to six-pound (nineteen and a half
pounds in 1962 is record) gray species. The gray is found from New
England to Georgia, and sometimes beyond to Florida; the spotted,
from Maryland to Mexico. Both are school fish and roam coastal
beaches and inlets, inland tidal sounds and rivers—over grassy bottoms particularly, where they feed upon shrimps and minnows mainly
—and over oyster bars and other shell reefs.

There are about a half dozen additional members of the *Cynoscion*
family.

The multi-member and easily confused **grouper** family (*Myctero-
perca, Epinephelus,* etc.) includes the strong and stubborn **Nassau
grouper** (*E. striatus*), the **red grouper** (*E. morio*) and the **black**
(*M. bonaci*). These are found, to varying degree, from the Canal
Zone to Massachusetts, via the West Indies and Texas. Most are Atlantic fish. Two of the groupers, at least, are found in the Pacific,
from Panama to Lower California. These are the **golden** (*M. para-
dalis*) and the **spotted cabrilla** (*E. analogus*).

Size can vary greatly. The average grouper runs from perhaps two
to ten pounds, but weights in excess of 100 are not uncommon. The
Nassau, red and black groupers seem to be taken most often by sport
fishermen. These bottom feeders like to feed over reefs, and hide in
rocky holes.

The Saltwater Basses

The familiar little (one- to four-pound) **sea bass** of the Atlantic coast (*Centropristes striatus*) likes to bottom-feed on crustaceans and smaller fish, over wrecks and reefs.

The **California kelp bass** (*Paralabrax clathratus*) of that state and Lower California (Mexico) is both a ready striker and fighter. It frequents coastal grass growths and eight to ten pounds is a record catch.

A close look-alike to the kelp bass is the **California sand bass** (*P. nebulifer*), a somewhat smaller fish of the same range that prefers sandy bottoms.

The **channel bass,** or red drum (*Sciaenops ocellatus*), can be a surf caster's delight, in average sizes three to ten pounds, from New York to Texas, although it is not unusual to take these ocean bass in thirty- to fifty-pound sizes in the Carolinas. Readily identified by a conspicuous black spot on its tail, it is called redfish in Florida, where it swims in the same water as the bonefish, and is often taken on flies by bonefishermen as it feeds in shallow salt bays.

The so-called **California white sea bass** (*Cynoscion nobilis*), or corbina (already mentioned), is not a true bass, but a spotless member of the weakfish family. This stubborn fighting fish is found from Mexico to Alaska and comes in sizes to about ten pounds when caught in the surf, around kelp beds and in coastal rivers (sometimes far up these).

Striped bass (*Roccus saxatilis*) are sometimes called rockfish. These gamey fighters roam both the Atlantic and Pacific coasts in sizes two to ten pounds, average, but often twenty or more (forty-six- to fifty-seven-pound record stripers were caught in the 1960s, in Maryland, Massachusetts and Oregon). The North Carolina to Massachusetts, and the San Francisco Bay and Coos Bay (Oregon) areas are particularly good.

This multi-striped (horizontally) silver fish was successfully introduced to California waters from New Jersey in 1879. It follows ocean beaches, likes rocky shores and points, and enters salt bays and rivers to spawn. It travels in offshore schools, often feeding voraciously at the surface upon bait fish (watch the birds!).

The **giant sea bass** (*Promicrops itaiara*), also called Warsaw grouper and Florida jewfish, roams from the Canal Zone to Florida, via the West Indies, on the Atlantic side, and north to the Gulf of California on the Pacific coast. This big, sluggish bottom-feeder measures his weight in the hundreds, even when young (the tackle record is 680, a Florida west coast fish taken in 1961). He likes to hang around offshore rocks, but will enter estuarine waters.

A somewhat smaller ocean giant is the **California black sea bass** (*Stereolepis gigas*), found from that state to Panama, in average sizes 150 to 250 pounds (the 1962 tackle record is 557, a Catalina Island, California, catch). Both these huge fish are edible.

Top-Feeding Saltwater Game Fish

The striped bass, already discussed, belongs here since it feeds in schools, at the sea's surface and in inland bays, as well as in the depths.

The **kingfish** (*Scomberomorus cavalla*), sometimes called king mackerel, is the largest of the mackerels, growing to more than eighty pounds (1963 tackle record in this country is a forty-four-pound Florida fish), but averaging perhaps five to fifteen. This fast and powerful game fish prowls from Panama to North Carolina, via the West Indies and Texas.

The **cero mackerel** (*S. regalis*) is found from Cape Cod to Florida and in the West Indies (notably Puerto Rico), usually in the vicinity of outer reefs, and in weight less than four pounds (although it may go several times that).

The **Spanish mackerel** (*S. maculatus*) is a school fish, like the others, but usually swims closer to shore, in sizes one to three pounds, average (record catches range from eight to thirteen pounds).

The swift and sporty **wahoo** (*Acanthocybium solandri*) ranges from the Mexican Pacific coast (i.e., Lower California, too) south to the Canal Zone, thence northward through the Caribbean to Texas, Florida, the Bahamas and on about as far as Maryland, in season. This loner is found near the surface of the open sea, also over reefs, in sizes about fifteen to twenty pounds, but can go much higher. (The 1962 world tackle record is a 149-pound Bahamas fish.)

The wahoo resembles a mackerel, but is not. It can be quickly identified by its long and low dorsal, of nearly even height throughout.

The **bluefish** (*Pomatomus salatrix*) swims worldwide, but only along the East Coast of North America—Nova Scotia to Florida and Texas. It averages two to six pounds, but has been taken to twenty-four (in 1953; an outstanding bluefish today would be one over twelve pounds).

When this tasty glutton is in a feeding frenzy, in an offshore school tearing up the surface, it will hit anything offered it. I've caught blues in the surf while using only a strip of white cloth on a hook.

The **dolphin** (*Coryphaena hippurus*), called dorado throughout its southern range, swims from Panama to Massachusetts on the Atlantic seaboard and to Oregon on the Pacific. This beautifully colored, blunt-headed blue water fighting fish with the long, sloping dorsal often resembles a living rainbow as it leaps magnificently from the ocean surface—usually in pursuit of flying fish. Look for this good-eating gamester about kelp beds, in the vicinity of the Gulf Stream "grass line" (floating seaweed), beneath planks, other flotsam.

This fish averages four to twenty-five pounds. The tackle record is over seventy-six, and a twenty-five- to thirty-pound dolphin is not a rarity.

The bonitos and tunas, of which there are several families, can also be classed as surface-feeding game fish, although the tuna, especially, does go deep—as you will discover if you hook one!

Both might be called mackerel types. The common **bonito** (*Sarda sarda*) runs in sizes one to six pounds (seldom over fifteen) and is edible, unlike some. It is found from New England to Texas.

Slightly larger, the oceanic, or **Arctic bonito** (*Katsuwonus pelamis*) is also called skipjack on the Pacific coast. It roams from New England through the West Indies, and from southern California to Panama.

The **albacore** (*Thunnus germo*) swims from Massachusetts to Puerto Rico and Alaska to Panama, and is a choice catch among the tunas, because of its white meat. It comes in sizes about ten to thirty-five pounds, has been taken to sixty-nine, in New Jersey waters, in 1961.

The edible **false albacore,** or little tuna (*Euthynnus alletteratus*), averages under five pounds, seldom exceeds fifteen, and is found from Cape Cod to the Gulf of Mexico and West Indies; also in Mexican and southern California waters; around rocks and in fast currents.

Another tuna, the **blackfin** (*Thunnus atlanticus*), resembles the albacore, but is a smaller fish, found from the Windward Islands (eastern Caribbean) to Bermuda, in one- to fifteen-pound sizes (record is forty-four and a half, for a South African catch). This fellow dives especially deep when hooked.

Several additional tuna will be discussed later, under big fish.

The **Pacific yellowtail** (*Seriola dorsalis*) swims from Panama to California and is noted for its tremendous initial run when hooked. To observe a school of these yellow-finned game fish tearing up a large area of the inland sea between Baja California and Mexico, in a feeding spree, is a sight to behold, indeed. A thirty- to forty-pound yellowtail is in the record class; five to twenty is average.

Sharing these warm waters with the yellowtail is *"el papagallo,"* the **roosterfish** (*Nematistius pectoralis*), with its high and strange dorsal fin. This swift fish swims at, or close beneath, the surface, over rocky and sandy inshore bottoms, and is a sheer delight for light tackle anglers who can get within casting range. This tropic torpedo averages ten to twenty pounds. A 114-pounder was taken in Mexican waters in 1960 (the world tackle record) and another, over fifty, in 1967.

Specialty Light Tackle Saltwater Game Fish

The **ladyfish,** or chiro (*Elops saurus*), is small—a three-pound catch of one of these graceful, big-eyed beauties would be considered large in Florida or Gulf of California (Mexican) waters—but what darting, high-leaping sport even such a small fish of this species can provide on light tackle, particularly the fly rod! This miniature tarpon moves into estuarine waters with the tide, to feed, mainly from North Carolina to Florida, and the Caribbean, and from northern Mexico southward in the Pacific.

Next to tarpon, the **snook,** or robalo (*Centropomus undecimalis*), is this writer's favorite light tackle fish. Old Linesides roams from Panama north, via Texas, to Florida, and, on the Pacific side, from Panama to Lower California. He comes in three- to ten-pound size, usually, although thirty-pounders are not uncommon in Florida. Look for him up in shallow rivers and bays, around mangrove roots, over both mud and sandy bottoms. The "snook" will not hesitate to use both his abrasive, toothless mouth or knife-sharp gill covers to part your line.

The mean-looking, pike-shaped **great barracuda** (*Sphyraena barracuda*) can satisfy both the light and heavy tackle enthusiast. He is called tiger of the sea—and looks it, with outthrust lower jaw and bristling teeth—but is actually quite timid of humans.

This two- to ten-pound fish (twenty- and thirty-pound 'cudas are not uncommon) can appear in a flash from out of nowhere, strike a lure and be on its way with incredible speed. In the Atlantic the great barracuda ranges north from Panama, throughout most of the Caribbean, to North Carolina, preferring outside reefs en route.

The **Pacific barracuda** (*S. argentea*) is smaller, about a foot in length, and offers considerably less sport. It swims from Panama to California and seldom exceeds twelve pounds.

The very fast and strong **permit** (*Trachinotus goodei*) is the largest of the pompano family. The world tackle record is fifty pounds, a Florida catch, but it averages less than half that size as it follows outside and inside reefs and open salt bays and sounds of the Carribean to Florida and North Carolina. Many expert anglers feel that the permit offers better sport than the bonefish.

The famed **bonefish** (*Albula vulpes*) is encountered from Panama through the Caribbean to Florida (with stragglers occasionally far beyond), and, on the Pacific side, northward to Mexico, perhaps southern California. These streamlined silver fish like to move in with the tide, onto estuarine shoals, to feed upon crustaceans. They average two to ten pounds; a fifteen-pound bone can be bragged about. Bonefish provide fine casting sport, particularly on flies.

The **tarpon** (*Tarpon atlanticus*), also called silver king—and worthy of the title—provides a worthy opponent for the most skilled light tackle angler. In North America old Big-Eye swims north from the Canal Zone in the Caribbean to Texas-Louisiana-Florida, and on to the Carolinas and sometimes beyond.

This heavy-bellied, chrome-plated high-jumper swims inshore along sandy beaches, over coastal reefs, and follows inflowing tides into muddy salt rivers and bays to feed upon mullet, pinfish and crabs. He comes in tiny two- and three-pound "fly rod" sizes to hundred-pounders (also taken on the fly rod!). The world tackle record is 238 pounds. What a great game fish!

The Deep Water Big Ones

The **Atlantic sailfish** (*Istiophorus americanus*) with its high, rainbow-hued dorsal fin, and its look-alike, the **Pacific sailfish** (*I. greyi*), both have an extended upper jaw, or "spear," as do the various marlins and the swordfish. These are all open-sea game fish, usually caught by trolling.

The Atlantic fish is found from Panama northward through the West Indies, and along the coasts of British Honduras, Mexico, Texas, Alabama, Florida—and beyond to the North Carolina area, sometimes farther, in sizes twenty-five to fifty pounds (world record is 141). The Pacific variety of these tail-walkers grows somewhat larger —the record is 221—and swims from Panama to southern California.

The **striped marlin** (*Makaira mitsukurii*) is confined to Pacific waters on our continent, ranging from Panama north to southern California. The record is 465 pounds; average is 150 to 250.

The **white marlin** (*Makaira albida*) is an Atlantic-side streak in the blue sea that ranges from Venezuela (where there seems to be the world's greatest concentration of these fish) northward throughout the West Indies to Florida and the Bahamas, the Carolinas and Maryland (where there is great sport off Ocean City) to Massachusetts. Size varies from about thirty to 160.

Atlantic blue marlin (*Makaira nigricans*) likewise follow this same route as the white marlin, but grow much bigger (the rod and reel 1968 record is 845 pounds, a Virgin Island fish). Even larger is the **Pacific blue marlin** (*M. mazara*), which ranges from Panama to the Gulf of California (Mexico), and a 1969 catch record for which stands at 1,153 pounds. And still larger than that is the **black marlin** (*M. indica*), a Pacific fish, the record for which is 1,560.

The **swordfish** (*Xiphias gladius*) has a flat sword extending from its upper jaw, instead of a rounded spear, like the others, and is said to be capable of a speed of seventy miles per hour! It is brown, instead of blue, and is found in southern California, Nova Scotia, New England and Cuban waters. (The Long Island to Nantucket area can be good for these broadbills.) The average weight is 200–300 pounds; the record, 1,182.

Bluefin tuna (*Thunnus thynnus*) annually follow the Bahamas-New York-New England-Nova Scotia migration route. These fish may weigh in excess of 1,000 pounds (the record is 1,040, taken in 1970) but they average fifty to 200.

Another tuna, the **Allison,** or yellowfin (*T. albacares*), swims from Panama to southern California and in the Atlantic from Maryland to Florida and on down through the West Indies, in sizes fifteen to over 100 pounds.

The **sawfish** (*Pristis pectinatus*) has a flat "saw," with large teeth along both edges, extending from its upper jaw. It is found from the Canal Zone to Texas, Florida and sometimes beyond to New Jersey. This fish, which may measure fifteen to twenty feet, is also found in the Pacific. The largest known catch at this writing is 736 pounds.

Sharks can also provide fine game fish sport, and they range in size from the familiar foot-long (and upward) **sand shark** to the great **white man-eater** (*Carcharodon carcharias*) that has been taken with rod and reel up to 2,664 pounds.

Sharks frequent North American waters, on all coasts, and the **mako** (*Isurus oxyrhynchus*) is considered by many anglers to provide the most sport (the mako averages around 750 pounds; the tackle record is 1,061). The **tiger shark** (*Galeocerdo cuvier*), taken to 1,780 pounds in 1964, off South Carolina; the **porbeagle** (*Lamna nasus*), to 430 pounds; and the **thresher shark** (*Alopias vulpinus*) are considered game fish. The thresher has been taken in sizes over 700 pounds. It can, and will, leap higher than a tarpon.

Chapter 6
Fishing from Shore

There are certain times when it is best for the angler to fish from shore. If the fish are feeding close in, for instance, a boat is not needed. In fact, the presence of a boat might even scare off the fish.

In San Francisco Bay careless, sometimes greedy anglers in boats repeatedly frighten away schools of striped bass, to the disappointment of other fishermen on shore who otherwise would have had a chance to catch some of these prized game fish. Even when he is fishing alone in a boat, an unthinking angler can succeed in making the fish stop biting by the noisy use of oars or motor, perhaps by the careless dropping of a tackle box or other object against the floor.

In rough weather an angler subject to seasickness will find it advantageous to fish from solid ground—provided the fish are striking within casting range. And the family man, of course, should never jeopardize his wife and children by taking them fishing in dangerous water.

It is cheaper to fish from shore, too. And often, should the fish refuse to co-operate, the shore angler's day need not be wasted. He can enjoy swimming, picnicking, camping and other diversions between bites.

On the other hand, without a boat your fishing range is limited. How frustrating it can be, for example, for a surf fisherman to observe a school of fish feeding beyond his casting range. Or perhaps the fish are near the opposite shore of a river that is too deep for him to wade.

Too, some of the most productive shorelines are difficult, if not impossible, to reach—save by boat. Such shores may have steep, dangerous slopes—often rocks. Or there may be crowding trees to make access and casting impossible.

The shorebound angler may have to walk, or drive, a considerable distance to find a good stretch from which to fish—only to discover this land posted against use by fishermen and hunters. Or, equally discouraging, I sometimes feel, a horde of eager anglers may be there already, standing shoulder to shoulder as they try to cast. Tempers can flare under such conditions as lines become tangled, fish are lost, etc. (*Photo 17.*)

The number of good shoreline fishing sites still available for public use continue to become sadly fewer each year. It is said, for instance, that only about 10 per cent of Florida's long, two-ocean coastline— the longest in the nation—is still available to the public. This is ironic, indeed, for our forefathers died for the right of free access to public waters, unhindered use of established thoroughfares, and so on.

It is generally recognized as the birthright of every American to enjoy freely that portion of any tidal beach lying between mean high and low tide lines. But how can a citizen enjoy what is rightfully his when careless legislators refuse to provide—for use by all—suitable access routes to the nearest public land? Should there not be a public street leading down to the water, it seems that the upland owners are invariably determined not to allow a citizen the privilege of crossing their property to reach such tidal water. Florida is notorious in this regard.

The shore fisherman should, of course, be able to distinguish between a promising shoreline and one that is best avoided. A good shore, as will be discussed in more detail later, is one that offers the fish food, safety and comfort. A bottom that is devoid of vegetation, rocks and other obstructions to provide these attractions—a shoreline that perhaps does not offer a stream that empties into the deeper water, to carry insects and other tidbits to waiting mouths—is one that the wiser angler shuns.

A shore need not be steep, or rocky, to prove dangerous—and the angler should remain aware of possible dangers even when casting from a relatively flat, innocent-appearing bank. There may be dangerous snakes, animals, even insects present. It is not difficult to step upon a rattlesnake or a water moccasin—the latter, especially, since they like to remain at the water's edge. And we all know—or should know —the danger of disturbed bees.

I recall the time I was fly fishing for rainbow trout down on the Katmai Peninsula of Alaska. I was accompanied by a guide, John Walatka, since departed for that Land of Endless Strikes. We were wading a swift river—John and I and another Alaskan guide, whom I recall only as Slim—and the trout were proving most co-operative: rising on all sides and frequently leaping clear of the water when hooked.

The riverbanks were covered with tall grass, and, in my excitement, I managed to fish my way around a point that hid me from the view of my friends. Only when Walatka came in search for me did I realize how far I had strayed.

"It's not a wise thing to get off by yourself like this—without a gun," my friend told me quietly. He eyed the thickly grassed bank for a moment and then added: "Come over here, I want to show you something."

We emerged from the water and he showed me an area of recently flattened grass that was about the size of a full bedspread. "Brown bear," John announced shortly. "He probably was lying here as you approached."

Later, my scalp prickled at the memory when I learned that Alaska brown, or Kodiak, bears grow to weights of 2,000 pounds, that a big male can bite his "tree mark" (to identify his range) twelve feet above ground, and outdistance a fast horse in the first hundred yards of a chase!

Incidentally, the second guide, Slim, had gotten snowed in in the bush the winter before for a considerable period. While thus confined he had managed to misplace his dentures. Undaunted, and with typical Alaska resourcefulness, Slim had carved himself a temporary set of false teeth from antler horn. He did such an expert job that his dentist, in Anchorage, offered him a job!

Done properly, fishing from shore can provide many happy hours. One of the greatest thrills is "sound casting" to schools of striped bass and other game fish that venture into inshore shallows at night to feed. Here the angler has only his ears to tell in which direction to cast— and how far. (Use a light and you will quickly scare away the fish.)

What a thrill it can be to make an accurate decision and immediately feel the weight of a struggling fish at the end of your line.

In conclusion, whether he fishes by night or by day, the good shore fisherman does not trespass. Ask permission first should there be any question. If you are refused, go elsewhere.

Chapter 7
How to Wade

There will be those times when the reader must either wade or forget about fishing. Often a promising stream will have banks too heavily grown to permit casting from shore. The dense growths may make it impossible to launch a boat, even a small one. Or the water may be too shallow to permit use of a boat. Or there may be too many rocks, or other obstructions, in the water to justify use of such a craft.

Too, the current may be too swift for an angler, fishing alone, to maneuver a boat should he wish to cast along a shoreline. Again, the proposed fishing site may be too distant to justify trailering a boat.

When such conditions prevail you must enter the water bodily. This can be tricky—even dangerous. If the water is shallow, a pair of rubber boots will suffice. But few situations can prove more annoying to an angler far from camp than a bootful of chill water! So, if you plan to fish the deeper streams and pools, chest-high waders will be required. (See *Photo 18.*)

Several kinds of boots and waders are available. Instead of the long-familiar, all-rubber hip boot, I prefer the newer and considerably lighter kind that employ a conventional rubber boot foot, the remainder being rubberized canvas that extends upward to crotch height. This boot folds readily, hence is easier to pack, too.

Waders, the better quality ones, are also made from such rubber-impregnated canvas. This material is carried upward to chest height from a calf-high, all-rubber boot. The inseam is usually of gum rubber, too, for better wear. A storage pocket, with flap, is often positioned at the top of the wader, in front, for storage of small items.

Both boots and waders come in either leg-hugging or loose-fitting styles. Some anglers prefer the snug fit type. Sometimes this boot has an adjustable strap, inside, that snaps firmly into position about the calf of the leg, better to hold the boot in position. Such a boot seems to offer less resistance to swift current, hence calls for less effort by the angler to remain erect. Boots and waders of this type also cling to the feet better, some users claim, thereby making walking easier on land.

The loose-fitting variety, on the other hand, are easier to remove after a tiring day—or, before that, should you fall into the water, before the fishing day is over.

Some boots and waders are made of very thin rubber, plastic, and nylon. This is done to make them both lighter and cheaper. However, these materials are more apt to puncture and tear than pure gum rubber, or rubber-impregnated canvas. Hence their limits should be recognized before purchase. Always buy the best foot gear that you can afford.

One can also purchase a lightweight wader that comes without the customary all-rubber boot foot permanently attached. This so-called "stocking foot" wader is intended to be worn inside wading shoes. These shoes may resemble heavy canvas sneakers, or hobnailed leather shoes, depending upon the type you select. You may, of course, substitute conventional shoes—canvas or leather—but these do not work as well. If you attempt to wear a stocking foot wader without protective shoes of some sort, the light sole material will soon wear through and leak.

Many anglers who live in warm climates, as I do, choose not to bother with waders. In my own case, for example, I simply wear a pair of old duck pants, canvas wading shoes (I'm not above using conventional sneakers, if I have to), a long-sleeved shirt and broadbrimmed hat (to safeguard against sunburn) and a belt type tackle case. After the fishing is over, these are replaced with dry garments and shoes for the drive home. (See *Photo 19.*)

There will be times, of course, when such an outfit is not practical, even though the water is warm and comfortable. In certain Florida areas, for instance, we have a tiny water bug that causes skin irritation. Again, there are those areas, sad to say, where anglers must fish in polluted water, or not fish.

The wading angler—especially the man working a fast and potentially dangerous stream—is often subject to sudden falls. This can result in a soaked wallet, lost glasses, perhaps even a choice rod hopelessly splintered. Even worse, there may result painful body bruises, even broken bones—or death from drowning, if the hapless angler should be swept into a deep pool, or carried over a falls. Should the weather be chill, he will be lucky to escape with a bad cold.

To avoid such unhappy circumstances, of course, one must remain on his feet. But this can be difficult when you are obliged to step from one slime-covered rock to the next. Perhaps, in order to reach a point where you can cast to a rising trout, you must wade over loose bottom stones that have been polished glass-smooth by years of water movement. Under such conditions the usual corrugated rubber boot or wader soles can slide hopelessly.

For many years anglers have sought means to reduce such risks. Some strap metal cleats over their rubber boots. Others wear heavy hobnailed leather shoes. The best prevention that has evolved so far, however, is the sole of compressed felt. This soft material does not wear out nearly so fast as one might at first fear. And it permits one to wade where previously even brave men would fear to tread. Felt-soled boots, waders and wading shoes cost more, but the additional investment is well justified.

(*Note:* In the Appendix the reader is shown how to make his own inexpensive felt-soled wading shoes, should a low fishing budget warrant this.)

Whether you wade in felt or ordinary soles, remember this important rule: avoid long steps that may end with your body being off balance. When the firmness of the bottom is questionable, slide one foot at a time cautiously forward. Feel your way. Make certain the first foot is firmly planted before raising the second.

Should the water before you be questionable—too murky, perhaps —don't take a chance. Detour. Call upon your own experience, and that of other waders. A swift current, for example, will often wash out a deep hole before a large rock. Conversely, it likely will have deposited the washed-out sand, and other debris, behind the rock, creating a shoal area there. So try to cross there, instead.

Avoid the risky practice of jumping from one rock or log to the next, unless you are *sure* you can make it. Mountain goats can do this. But they are better equipped. And they don't do it while wearing boots or waders. A broken leg, even a badly sprained ankle, very likely will not only ruin your vacation, but also prevent your return to work.

Don't be ashamed to cut yourself a wading staff (or buy one). It is surprising how helpful one of these wading aids can prove—even should it be only a short stick cut for the purpose. The staff can also be used as a probe, to determine depths waiting in your path.

(Where to wade—whether upstream or down, near points or in coves, and so on—will be discussed in detail in later chapters.)

The wading fisherman should wear comfortable clothing that fits loosely and is lightweight. Wool, or heavy cotton, socks will allow your feet to "breathe." This is important. If the weather is cold, wear silk or nylon socks inside these—and suitable long underwear. Insulated lightweight underwear is available for very cold weather, as are down-filled pants and jackets. Some anglers prefer to provide their feet additional cold weather protection by wearing insulated—or so-called "thermal"—boots and boot-foot waders.

A fishing vest (or a long-sleeved fishing jacket, for cold weather) will come in handy while wading. These garments provide a number of pockets for storage of spare tackle that should be carried with you when you wade. A couple of the pockets should be large enough to accept a plastic lure box, or wallet. And, since creels seem to have gone out of style, the fishing vest or jacket should provide washable storage space for those fish you decide to keep.

Ideally, this "game pocket" should be of snap-in or zipper-holding design, so it can be removed for separate washing and drying. I like to carry a lightweight rubberized nylon fishing shirt, complete with hood, in this "creel" pocket—in case I should get caught in a sudden shower. My lunch often goes there, too.

After a man loses a few good fish he appreciates the value of having a landing net available while wading, cumbersome though this item may prove at times. Such a net should be lightweight, with aluminum bow and handle, and mesh pocket about two feet deep. Some anglers like to use adjustable (telescoping) handles; others, a net with short hardwood handle that is attached to the belt (with a snap) via an elastic cord that stretches several feet.

I've seen anglers capable of expertly disabling a thrashing fish by gripping it firmly in the lower gills with the free hand. Others carry a small belt gaff. (The point is a constant threat, however, and you must try to keep it covered with a cork, etc.) But I prefer the safer, easier to use, net.

In conclusion, let me emphasize again the need for constant safety awareness while wading—particularly if you should be fishing alone. It is not unusual, for instance, for a Florida wader to invite risk by towing behind him, in the customary manner, a floating stringer of freshly caught fish. Joe Brooks, a young tackle store operator at Melbourne Beach, will vouch for this.

Brooks and a buddy were wading—spinning for seatrout—on the Indian River flats recently. It was spring, a period of the year when large sharks, mostly hammerheads, swim in hungrily through inlets to spread out over estuarine shoals to feed upon stingrays. Brooks watched one of these brutes approach him to investigate the several live weakfish which the angler trailed behind him from a fifteen-foot nylon cord attached to his belt.

Brooks recognized that he was in an awkward position. Shortly before, he and his friend had felt obliged to seek safety in their anchored skiff when another shark had come close. Since then, however, the other man, too, had waded away from the boat. And now the advancing shark was in a position between Joe Brooks and the skiff.

The endangered fisherman glanced about nervously. He was some four hundred yards from shore. The muddy bottom of the chest-deep salt water was too soft for quick movement. Brooks decided to try and reach the comparative safety of a small tripod steel tower nearby —a device customarily used to mark a leased oyster bed.

The young fisherman managed to reach this object ahead of the approaching shark. He could see the brute clearly now. It appeared to be about eleven feet long. Brooks hugged the marker, meanwhile lifting his stringer of fish from the water.

"That big devil came within six feet of me—I thought that at any second I might lose a leg," Brooks told me later. "But I remained very still . . . and after about ten minutes, he left."

Inland, of course, there are no sharks. Yet an angler might wade out safely to a vantage casting point in some mountain stream only to have a small avalanche of limbs, stumps and other flotsam descend upon him unexpectedly—to tear his waders, perhaps even topple him into the water—the runoff of some unseen storm upstream! Or perhaps he is fishing downstream from one of the many power impoundments scattered throughout the nation. Should the floodgates be suddenly opened, as they often are, he will find himself confronted with a crest of several additional feet of water that he had not reckoned for.

So be alert to danger—always—while wading.

Chapter 8
Fishing with a Boat

A boat, of course, can spare an angler concern for sudden high water, treacherous bottoms, impossibly dense shorelines, and similar problems that can plague the wading fisherman. The man in a boat need not worry nearly so much about dropping a lure into the water, when it becomes necessary to change one; or where to store his lunch until midday; or where to sit down.

Fishing boats come in a variety of sizes, purchase costs and rental fees (see *Photos 20–22*). The once popular Northwoods canoe has been largely replaced by the small outboard skiff, or perhaps a rented rowboat with the angler's own motor fastened to its transom.

Some traveling fishermen like the portability afforded by the small inflatable fishing craft that are available. A couple summers ago my wife and I took a rubber dinghy aboard our motor home as we drove north to the end of the Alaska Highway, fishing otherwise inaccessible water as we traveled. (*Photo 23.*)

Still other anglers prefer craft of special design to meet special needs. Recently, for example, there appeared on the market several outboard boats that are ideal for the sportsman who finds it necessary to fish alone (something I do not recommend). Such a craft is controlled from an elevated bucket seat near the bow. This position permits the operator to "work" (cast) a shoreline at slow speed, without the need for an assistant to keep the boat within casting range.

Those who can afford it may purchase custom-built fishing craft designed to their own specifications. Perhaps the finest of these I've been aboard is owned by expert Florida saltwater fly fisherman Al Pflueger, Jr., of Miami. Al designed his twenty-three-foot oceangoing, twin-inboard-motored formula hull so there would be only one small console, aft, protruding above the deck to interfere with his fly casting and fish battling activities. And even this structure has rounded edges, thereby offering least chance of snagging a line.

The man who does not own his own fishing boat, or who cannot borrow one, will be obliged to rent a craft. Rowboats are usually available for five dollars, or less, per day—whereas small outboard skiffs may cost three times that much, depending upon the locale. To charter a sport-fishing cruiser, with captain and mate, for ocean sport, expect to pay about a hundred dollars per day. Should this sum exceed your budget, you have the alternatives of either sharing such expense—and fishing space in the boat—with others, or you can sail aboard one of the coastal "headboats" that may carry twenty-five or more anglers at a time, with the individual rate reduced accordingly. (At some Florida coastal cities this headboat rate is seven dollars per person, all day, with the boat operators providing your tackle.)

Do you know how to operate a boat safely? From the moment you cast off the lines, you will be responsible for everyone aboard. If you cannot meet this important responsibility, you had better prepare yourself beforehand! To wait could be too late.

Is your craft overloaded? Have you taken too many passengers aboard? (This is one of the most common causes of difficulty afloat.) If you cannot tell by inspection, there should be a small metal plate mounted somewhere inside the boat, placed there by the builder, to tell what weight the craft can safely carry. Or you can apply this formula, recommended by the Outboard Boating Club of America:

Multiply the boat's length times its maximum width, times the maximum depth, times 0.6, then divide by 12, and multiply by 150 (except where the beam measurements are 48 inches, use 19 inches as maximum depth; for 49- to 52-inch beams use 20 inches as maximum depth; 53- to 56-inch beams use 21 inches as maximum depth; 57 inches or over use 22 inches as maximum depth). See *Figure 8–1*.

There are other responsibilities, too. There should be at least one anchor aboard, with sufficient anchor rope to reach bottom, and prevent the boat from drifting helplessly, should the motor fail. There should be an approved type life jacket available for each person, yourself included. Don't assume that these and other items are aboard, just because you rented, or perhaps borrowed, the boat in good faith. Check and make sure, before leaving the dock; refer to *Figure 8–2*.

Silly though it may seem, "running out of gas" accounts for much of the difficulty experienced by otherwise intelligent persons. I recall the time that I and several other experienced Florida boatmen were stunned by what we saw taking place at a public boat launching ramp. A young father had driven up with his wife and two children. Behind them they trailered a gleaming new outboard cabin cruiser.

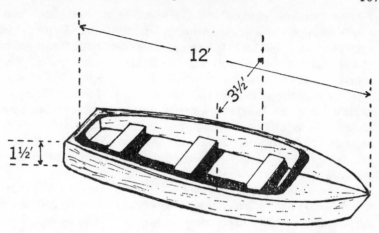

Figure 8–1 (Courtesy of Louisiana Game Commission)

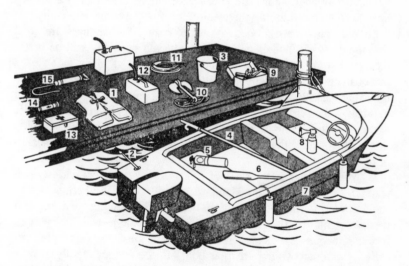

Figure 8–2 Safety Check List: (1) Approved lifesaving device for each person, (2) Proper lighting (light not required if boat is not operated after dark), (3) Bailing bucket, (4) Boat hook, (5) Fire extinguishers, (6) Paddle or oars, (7) Fenders, (8) Horn or whistle, (9) Tool kit, (10) Anchor, (11) Line, (12) Gasoline cans (spare), (13) First-aid kit, (14) Flashlight, (15) Bilge pump (Courtesy of Colorado Div. of Game, Fish & Parks)

It soon became obvious that the would-be captain wasn't quite sure how to go about getting his craft into the water. So we helped him. Then came the shock. He stepped aboard, carrying the six-gallon gasoline tank. Since this tank was still inside its cardboard shipping carton, we had to assume that it was empty.

It was. And the motor failed to start, of course. Meanwhile, he had already cast off his lines, and was now drifting helplessly! One of us had to go after him and tow him back to dock. Meanwhile, we explained to the young boat owner that the tank should be filled with gas, and the motor started—to make certain it is functioning properly —before casting off.

If you are using an outboard type engine, you should be able to tell at a glance whether it is too large, or too small, for the boat. There is little to be gained by overpowering a rowboat, or a small skiff, when a ten-horsepower engine is all that may be required. Not only will the too large power plant make the small craft ride bow-high, at high speed it may actually lift the entire boat out of the water! Passengers have been thrown out into the water this way—on turns, especially.

Should you swamp a boat, try not to panic. The chances are good that the craft will not sink. If it does not, you probably will be better off by remaining with it. It has been found that as many as a dozen persons can be safely supported by clinging to a sixteen-foot wooden boat that has filled with water. Most metal boats, too, will float when capsized—the result of seat air tanks, or other built-in provision for flotation. Often it can prove farther to the nearest shore than you may think. So consider the matter carefully before you swim off in search of help.

Do you understand the rules of rights-of-way on rivers and in open waters? Do you know the standard coloring and numbering system for buoys and other navigational aids? How about distress and weather signals? Would you be able to employ the proven best way to rescue someone who has fallen overboard; or know the safest place to bring him aboard your particular boat? If you cannot readily answer these and similar important boating questions, you will do well to contact your nearest Coast Guard Auxiliary, U. S. Power Squadron or Red Cross unit. Even "experienced" boatmen have been surprised how much they could learn from the courses in small boat operation that are provided by these organizations, usually at no charge. You will learn that it is illegal to create a wake hazardous to anchored, or docked, boats you may pass, for example. You will be taught other

18. Chest-high waders keep the water out of this fisherman's clothes.

19. A well-attired fisherman protects himself against the elements.

20. A canoe on a river.

21. A typical outboard skiff.

22. A custom-rigged fishing boat for deep sea fishing.

23. A rubber dinghy is extremely useful for otherwise inaccessible waterways.

24. Deep sea fishing with natural bait.

25. In the background is this fisherman's electronic depth indicator.

26. A young fisherman holds his catch.

27. The safest way to gaff a fish is to bring the sharp hook quickly upward into the fish's stomach about midway between tail and head.

28. The next three shots are of the overhead spin-cast grip. Grasp the rod so the reel support is positioned with two fingers of the rod hand on each side. The thumb is on top to aid in controlling the cast.

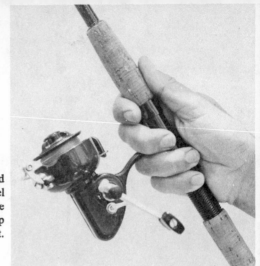

29. With the other hand turn the reel handle forward until the line collector guide is closest to the underside of the rod.

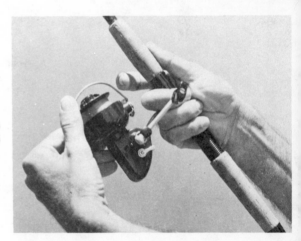

30. Hold the line clear as you remove your other hand from the reel handle and reach forward to push the reel's wire bail downward, thereby locking it in casting position out of the way.

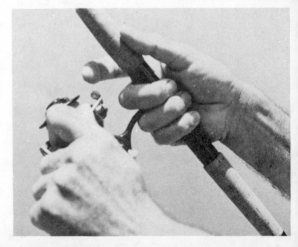

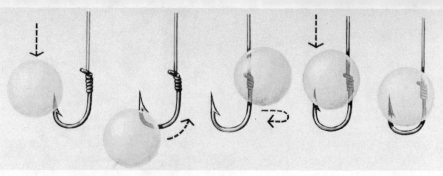

31. A. Salmon eggs are fragile and should be positioned on the hook carefully, using the steps shown above.

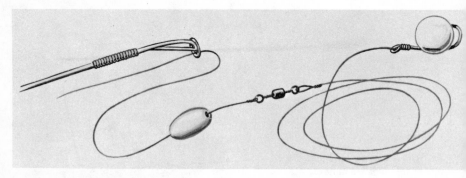

B. How a terminal rig with egg-type sinker can be used.

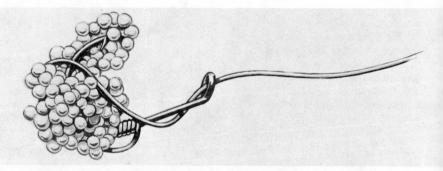

C. Anglers sometimes use small egg sacs to hold the cluster to the hook.

important things: like the exercise of courtesy and common sense while in a boat.

There are several ways one can fish from a boat. So-called "still fishing" is probably the most popular method. To do this you need only anchor your craft at a site where you have reason to believe that fish are present. You then lower a baited hook and wait for action. When the action is slow some anglers attract fish to the site by chumming. (See Chapter 14.)

You can also cast natural bait, or artificial lures, from an anchored boat (see *Photo 24*). For casting, my choice is for but two persons to occupy a rowboat or small outboard skiff. If necessary, a third person can be present, but he should occupy himself only with operating the boat. (When bottom fishing, three persons can fish from such a craft.)

If but two men are fishing, they can take turns at the controls. Both anglers can fish, of course, if they are willing to let the boat drift. Drift fishing has become popular, both beneath and above the surface (i.e., casting).

Sometimes two men can fish simultaneously while trolling from a small boat. One will be handicapped, however, since he must guide the boat while holding his rod, too. Rod holders can be purchased that will hold an unattended rod at the gunwale position. When this method of trolling is used the reel drag should be set as lightly as possible—to give the rod owner time to grasp the stick. Set the tension too tightly, and a striking fish is apt to break the line, even pull the rod overboard. It happens regularly.

Trolling will be described in detail in Chapter 16: what tackle is required for various kinds of trolling; how to determine the proper speed for pulling real or artificial baits through the water from a boat that is under way; and so on.

An electronic depth indicator (*Photo 25*) can be a big help when fishing strange waters where the bottom is uneven and subject to abrupt shoaling. This device can also be used to reveal the presence of fish below—schooled fish, usually—should you consider it sporting to fish this way. The Appendix describes how such instruments operate.

State law requires that your boat—depending upon the size of its engine (ten horsepower, or more, in Florida)—must be registered, for a fee, much like your automobile. Proof of ownership of the boat (i.e., a title) must be presented before a registration certificate will be issued. Numbers of a specific size, corresponding to the registration certificate number, must then be affixed to the bow before the boat can be operated.

Chapter 9
The Hand Line and Cane Pole

When the world's first angler—whoever he was—caught the first fish —whatever it was—we must assume that he did so with a hand line. Prior to that, when hunger drove him to do so, the primitive man may have scooped fish from the shallows with his bare hands. Or possibly he trapped them against a crude barricade. Perhaps he used his spear to impale the quarry in the shallows. But to *catch* a fish, in the sense that we speak of angling today, the first angler had to conceive the baited hook, with line attached.

The method has not changed since. True, the first crude hook— likely it was merely a splinter of bone or shell, perhaps a sharp piece of chipped stone—has been improved considerably since then. So has the original "line" of dried vine, or animal tendon, or intestine, or whatever. But anglers still use the hand line, and quite effectively, too. It may surprise you to learn that there are commercial fishermen throughout the world who catch more fish, and faster, by hand line than could the most expert rod and reel angler, were he to try and compete.

The main advantage of the hand line is its portability. You can carry in a pocket the necessary amount of line, with its associated terminal equipment. Or you can easily tuck it away in your luggage, or the glove compartment of your car, ready for quick use. I am reminded of the many letters of appreciation from servicemen stationed throughout the world that I discovered in the voluminous files of my friend Bo Randall, of Orlando, Florida, maker of the world-famous Randall sporting, combat and survival knives. The last mentioned blades have hollow handles inside which can be carried fishing lines, water purification tablets and similar items for emergency use by jungle fighters, downed airmen and so on. Lost fliers, floating on the sea in their rubber rafts while awaiting rescue, have blessed Randall as they used the simple, yet effective, fishing tackle inside their knife handles to catch enough food to survive. The original Astronauts carried similar knives, made by Randall to their specifications.

Such simple fishing equipment also has the advantage of being inexpensive. It costs so little, in fact, that there can be no excuse for not outfitting every youthful member of the family. All one needs is a few yards of line, a hook, sinker and small bobber, to discover the priceless joys of fishing in the healthful outdoors.

I recall how I learned to fish with such a basic rig, quite a number of years ago, in the quiet pool below the splashing mill dam of the big lake at Manahawkin, New Jersey. I and other grade school boys would assemble on the banks there in the evening, when the air was soft and warm, and fireflies often flitted carefree through the settling dark. We would heave out our earthworm-baited hooks, each supported just above the bottom by a cork salvaged from some old bottle, then settle back expectantly to wait for the fun to start. To see, and feel, those millpond catfish strike again and again, leaving widening rings of bobber ripples each time, was exciting, indeed.

Sometimes, as we hurried to disengage a wriggling catch from the hook, our slimy fingers would slip. The catfish would swing its blunt head vengefully from side to side, and we would get "horned," by its ice-pick-sharp fins. How that could hurt!

One disadvantage of the hand line, of course, is the fact that there is no reel brake available to spare your fingers from becoming "burned" by the outgoing line as you try to handle a big fish. Also, it may prove difficult to heave your line out far enough, and bring it back in, when necessary, without becoming snagged or tangled. The man worming for trout from an overgrown stream bank, for instance, will have difficulty getting his bait out. And there may be grass or other aquatic growths extending outward a sufficient distance from the shore to snag his terminal rig and make retrieving difficult, if not impossible.

Under such circumstances it will help if the angler cuts himself a long willow, or other, switch to serve as a fishing pole, after first tying the near end of his line to the tip. Most of us have seen a picture or painting of a typical barefoot farm boy with such a homemade rod. Dressed in worn overalls and broad-brimmed hat, the youth saunters down a tree-lined country lane, proudly carrying the homemade stick over one shoulder, while his small stringer of panfish dangles from the other hand.

It is usually easier to use a pole made of cane. Such a fishing pole can be purchased quite reasonably at the local tackle or hardware store. (A sixteen-foot, varnished cane pole costs about $1.50.) I must confess that for years I felt only a secret pity for persons obliged to fish thus. Then I moved to the Deep South and the black people there initiated me to the relaxed joys of cane poling.

There is something beautifully simple about this kind of fishing. You might say that, in his own way, the cane poler is quite as much an expert as the master dry fly caster. Much as the flyman is capable of placing his delicate offering with both extreme accuracy and grace of movement, so the veteran cane poler can usually foretell with incredible exactness what it is that is nibbling at his bait, and—by carefully observing the behavior of the twitching bobber—predict just what is going to happen next.

It is customary to keep a hand line wrapped upon a short stick, or a small wooden frame of some sort (such a support usually comes with the line when you purchase it). With a cane pole, however, the line need be only slightly longer than the pole—about eighteen or twenty feet—and when the pole is not in use the line can be kept wrapped about it in loose spirals, then secured at the butt end.

Figure 9–1 shows a typical hand line or cane pole terminal rig. The float is used to support the hook and small sinker—if one is used—at a depth that will give best results. Usually, this is just above the bottom, so the fish will be able readily to see the offering.

Another advantage of the float is that it gives an immediate indication that a fish is fooling with the bait. Thus an amateur angler—one who otherwise might not be prepared to set the hook in time—will be given ample warning to do so.

As the illustration also shows, floats come in a variety of sizes and shapes. They are usually made of hollow plastic, since this material is more durable than cork or balsa, which may also be used. Most floats have a center hole through which the line may be passed and secured by inserting a peg into the hole, to wedge the line fast. Some floats, however, require that the line be fastened to them externally.

Hooks used for hand line and cane pole fishing will usually be small —perhaps from No. 12 up to about No. 4—since the cane poler expects to mainly catch panfish (although this is not always the case). Baits, likewise, will be largely those used to take the smaller fish: doughballs for catfish, and so on, as discussed in Chapter 3.

In conclusion, don't make the mistake of looking down upon those who enjoy using cane poles, even hand lines. Try it, you may like it.

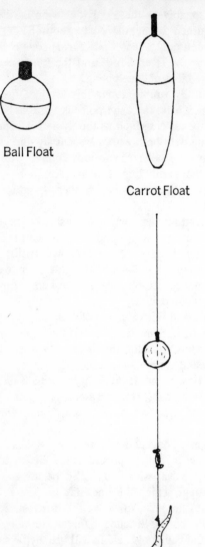

Ball Float

Carrot Float

Teardrop Float

Figure 9–1

too. I've seen commercial sea trout (weakfish) anglers fill their skiffs nearly to the sinking point—and rapidly, at that—while using such simple poles in Florida Bay, in the vicinity of Sand Key. These hard-working men would employ the same rhythm, over and over: the shrimp-baited hook is cast out by bringing the long cane pole forward, in an overhead arc, to slap the bait against the surface. The cork is then immediately "popped" (pulled under noisily) a time or two—this to attract the sea trout's attention. When the strike comes the hooked fish is lifted quickly into the boat, removed, and the action is commenced anew—almost with the same motion.

Chapter 10
Bait and Spin Casting (and Fishing)

"Bait casting" is also called "plug casting"—and neither description is adequate. (Reason: both baits and plugs can also be cast with other tackle, spinning tackle, for instance.) A better expression might be "revolving reel casting," since this is what mainly distinguishes so-called bait and plug casting tackle from the other kinds.

As mentioned in Chapter 1, bait casting rods usually measure between five and six feet in length, a few being shorter, some longer. The action of such rods—the shaft's degree of stiffness, or ability to bend backward and forward from the vertical, or at-rest, position when used to cast a bait or lure—may vary from very light (i.e., a whippy tip) to heavy (a stiff stick), depending upon the weight of the bait or lure that is to be cast.

Some anglers prefer a combination whippy (or so-called "fast") tip, to handle light lures, and a stiff butt section to provide the backbone to handle heavy fish.

This brings us once more to the term "balanced tackle." Try casting a light lure with a too stiff rod, or a heavy lure with a too limber rod, and you will soon appreciate the need for such carefully chosen tackle. Again, there is no point in installing a small reel on a big rod. The heavy line intended for use with the big rod would not only fill up the little reel too soon, but would likely spring outward from the tiny spool in stiff coils, to cause a snarl.

One becomes an accomplished bait caster only after considerable practice—and only a well-balanced outfit that permits easy, almost effortless casting will prevent the beginner from becoming discouraged while he learns.

The sole aim in casting, of course, is to drop the bait or lure within striking range of a fish—or, at least, at a spot where you hope a fish might be present. This calls for good casting form and an educated thumb to slow the revolving reel spool to a halt at just the right time. Drop your offering short of the target area, or go too far beyond it, and the fish likely will remain unaware of its presence. Drop it too close, and you may scare away the quarry.

Another thing: if you fail to maintain just the right thumb pressure while casting, the rapidly revolving reel spool is apt to overrun itself. It is this turning at a rate faster than line is leaving the spool that causes a backlash, or "bird's nest."

A body of water without shoreline obstructions that might snag your line, is a good place to practice casting. Any reasonably spacious area on land, however—your front lawn, for example—will also do. You should use a target of some kind, to measure your improvement. For water practice a skish ring, or an inflated bike tire, even a small floating board, if necessary, will suffice. On land you can settle for a weighted-down newspaper.

Proper timing is the big thing in any form of casting. Should there be a casting club in your area, the members very likely will be happy to help you without charge. You can also seek assistance from anglers who know how to cast; from tackle store dealers, and others. If there is no one to assist, you can still learn how to cast effectively by following the instructions given here.

I would recommend use of a bait casting rod that has a recessed (lowered) reel seat, as shown in *Photo 1* of Chapter 1. A rod with a straight handle does not permit easy "thumbing" of the revolving reel spool. With this style of rod one's thumb has to be raised higher to make contact with the reel.

Overhead Bait Cast

Let us assume that you have available a rod with action suitable for casting a five-eighths-ounce, hookless practice weight. (If necessary, a plug of comparable weight, after the hooks have been removed, will do, instead.) For proper balance, this rod will call for a quick-starting, light-running reel.

A full reel starts easier, and permits you to cast farther. It also is easier to brake, with the thumb, and permits a faster retrieve of the line. So fill the spool to within about a quarter inch of its capacity. Use 8 to 12 pound breaking test line, preferably a supple, braided line. Should you not have available that much good (strong) line to fill the spool, you can wind on first, instead, a hundred yards or so of old line. Or you can use a cork or plastic arbor in connection with such old backing line. (An arbor reduces the effective diameter, or line capacity of a revolving reel.)

To make the popular overhead cast, used by perhaps 90 per cent of all fishermen, grasp the bait casting rod handle comfortably with your right hand. (Reverse this procedure if you are left-handed.) Your thumb should rest against the line and the partly exposed spool flange. Your forefinger should be crooked about the finger hook, on the underside of the rod, should there be one.

The "click"—or reel ratchet—adjustment should be in the off position. (This very weak brake is used only to prevent line from slipping needlessly from the spool while the rod is being carried, or while it is being used for still fishing or trolling.)

Should the reel have a free-spooling control, set this so line can run off the spool unhindered. (Right now the pressure from your thumb will prevent this happening.)

If there is an anti-backlash device—i.e., a provision for adjusting tension upon the spool—adjust this so the weight of the practice plug will cause the plug to drop downward fairly easily from the tip of the horizontally extended rod, with no thumb pressure applied to the reel spool. (You likely will have to make a few casts before you find that anti-backlash adjustment that is best suited to your particular style of casting.)

Next, picture yourself standing before a large clock, the face of which is as tall as you. (See *Figure 10-1.*) Then, with the rod pointing toward the ten o'clock position, adjust the line so the practice plug dangles about six inches below the rod tip. (Some casters prefer a foot.) The rod tip should be pointing directly at, or perhaps slightly above, the spot where you wish the cast plug to land. Turn your wrist and forearm so the reel handles are pointing up. (They should remain that way throughout the cast that is about to follow.)

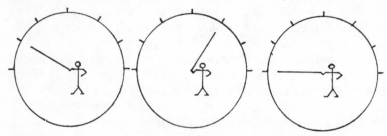

Figure 10-1

Now, with your right arm held comfortably close to your body, and the forearm parallel to water or ground, bring the rod up and back quickly—but smoothly—to about the vertical position. This is done by letting the wrist function as a moving pivot, the elbow as a fixed pivot. (The elbow, like the upper arm, remains in the same position throughout the cast.)

As you stop the rod briefly at the vertical, or twelve o'clock, position you will feel the momentum (weight) of the practice plug pull the limber rod back still farther—to about the one o'clock position, as shown. This flexing or "loading" of the rod is exactly what you want. It has stored in the rod the power that will be needed to shoot the plug forward.

Soon as you feel the rod fully loaded at the one o'clock position you must use your wrist to snap the rod forward until it points to about the ten-thirty o'clock position. At this point most of the braking (thumb) pressure is released from the reel spool. This allows the rod —like an unleashed spring—to hurl the plug toward its destination. Meanwhile, you are maintaining sufficient thumb pressure against the whirling reel spool to prevent it from overrunning itself, to cause a backlash.

By this time your forearm and wrist have dropped down, leaving the rod pointing toward the target and slightly above the horizon, as illustrated. As the plug approaches its target, increase thumb pressure to slow down the forward speed. Then, at the proper moment, brake the revolving spool to a halt, causing the plug to drop exactly where you want it to land.

(Even if your reel is equipped with an anti-backlash device, you must still use your thumb to stop the speeding plug at the right time.)

Obviously, this is a cast that must be practiced before you can become proficient. Don't make the mistake, as many bait casters do, of trying to *throw* the lure, as you might a baseball. Instead, a simple forward flip of the flexed rod is all that is needed.

You cannot hurry the action. Nor can you delay it. Strive for a smooth, pendulum-like timing throughout the cast. The rod is brought upward and backward. There is felt the telltale backward tug as the flying lure imparts its momentum (energy) to the now resisting rod. Then this power is directed forward, to shoot the lure smoothly on its way—somewhat like an arrow being released from a bow.

Other Bait Casts

After you have mastered the timing of the overhead cast you should find yourself able to use this knowledge, or "feel," to advantage in making other casts in those situations where the overhead approach is not feasible. Certain species of fish—snook, for example—habitually prowl close against dense, overhanging shores.

To hear—and not be able to see—several big robalo "tearing up" the shallows, darting and whirling and splashing as they feed upon bait fish, can be truly exciting. These fish may be feeding a dozen feet or more from the outer edge of the mangroves. To reach them you must cast your lure in such a way that it glides in low beneath the tangled branches, perhaps only a couple feet above the surface, to land amidst the fish. This is not possible with an overhead cast.

You must make a side cast, instead. This is merely an overhead cast executed with the rod tipped far to the right (or left) instead of being held vertically, as before. The degree of tipping will depend upon your ability to prevent the lure from striking the water before it reaches its destination.

As the beginner becomes more proficient he will discover that there are other casts which can be made to meet specific needs. For example, should there be obstructions present—both overhead and close at your right hand—you can hold your rod horizontally across your chest, with tip pointing left, and use a backhand cast to get the line out. Again, you may be standing at the end of a dock with overhanging roof, and casting obstructions on both sides. In that case you can use a flip cast. The rod tip is held straight down, then flipped straight away from you, with a snap of the wrist.

Some determined anglers will make the "bow and arrow" cast, when otherwise impossible casting conditions warrant this. Forcing his way through dense brush, the fisherman will stand near the water's edge to push his rod out through the growths. Then, holding on gingerly to the lure, to avoid becoming hooked by the barbs, he puts a sharp bow in the rod—by pulling against the hand-held lure. The lure is then released, causing the flexed rod to shoot the lure out over the water.

Overhead Spinning Cast

While this cast is made in the same manner as the overhead bait cast already described—that is, through the arc ten-one-ten o'clock— you are now using tackle that is quite different, and which requires a new technique. A spinning reel mounts below the rod, instead of atop it, and now you no longer need to shift the rod to the other hand in order to crank the reel. Now it is the forefinger of the rod hand, instead of the thumb, that applies braking pressure to line and revolving reel spool. And the spool does not turn during the cast. It revolves only when a fish succeeds in pulling line from it, after overcoming the resistance of the reel brake, or drag. Hence no danger of backlash.

To learn how to spin cast (it is much easier to master than bait casting) we will assume that we have available a balanced rod, reel and line: an outfit suitable for casting a practice plug, this time one about three eighths of an ounce in size.

Grasp the rod so the reel support, or leg, is positioned with two fingers of the rod hand on each side, as shown in *Photo 27.* The thumb, meanwhile, is on top, to aid in controlling the cast.

The practice plug should be hanging from six to twelve inches below the rod tip. Set to the off position the reel's anti-reverse control, should there be one. With your other hand turn the reel handle forward until the line collector guide is closest to the underside of the rod (see *Photo 28*), then reach down with tip of the rod hand forefinger and lift the line upward slightly from the collector guide. The line is not now touching any part of the bail.

Hold the line clear, thus, as you remove your other hand from the reel handle and reach forward to push the reel's wire bail (if there is one) downward, thereby locking it in casting position, out of the way, as shown in *Photo 29.*

(At this stage, should you be using a closed-face spinning reel, one which has no visible pickup mechanism, use your rod hand forefinger to hold the line tightly against the underside of the rod handle. Then crank the reel handle backward until it stops. This stopping indicates that the line pickup mechanism inside the reel has been disengaged, and the line is now free for casting.)

Now follow the procedure illustrated earlier (see *Figure 10–1*) for overhead bait casting. Hold the casting arm comfortably close to the body, and, with a smooth, pendulum-like movement of the wrist (only) bring the rod upward and backward from about the ten o'clock position—where it had been pointing at, or slightly above, the target. Halt the backstroke briefly at the vertical (directly overhead) point. Then flip the rod forward again immediately to the ten o'clock line release angle.

At this position the line is released simply by quickly straightening out the forefinger of the rod-holding hand. This allows the line to slip off the tip of this finger, where it had been held under tension in readiness for this moment. Complete the cast, meanwhile, by following through in the usual manner: drop the rod tip down to approximately the horizontal position. This gives the outgoing line maximum flight freedom.

Caution: let the line slip too soon from the tip of the forefinger, during the forward portion of the overhead spinning cast, and you send the plug sailing too high in the air: far above the target. Conversely, hold onto the line too long, and you will cast into ground, or water, close before your feet! Practice soon corrects such casting errors, however.

The line may be slowed down in its outward travel by extending the forefinger downward, to make light (brushing) contact with the coils of line leaping from the stationary reel spool. When you wish to stop the outgoing line, simply press the tip of the forefinger against the lip of the reel spool.

The outgoing line may also be stopped simply by using your free hand to move forward the reel handle. This causes the bail to snap to the closed position, and the line is simultaneously moved into "fish-fighting" position on the pickup roller. That is, assuming that the anti-reverse mechanism has been engaged, any line leaving the reel from this point on must first overcome the resistance of the reel's adjustable drag.

(If you are using a closed-face spinning reel and wish to stop the outgoing line—without turning the reel handle and engaging the gear mechanism to do so—you can use your forefinger to catch the line and press it against the underside of the rod handle.)

Other Spinning Casts

Backhand, "bow and arrow," and other special casts can usually be made easier with spinning tackle than they can with bait casting equipment, since the spinning rod is usually at least a foot longer. The circular, or "lariat," cast, for instance, is used by spin fishermen who discover themselves in a tight corner where normal rod movements are impossible. The circle cast is made by swinging the lure rapidly in a tight circle about the rod tip. When enough momentum has been developed, line is released and the lure sails out over the water, parallel to the shore. It is true that you are limited to but two casting directions when using this method. But otherwise, you would not be able to cast at all.

Spin Casting

This method of fishing should not be confused with straight spinning, although it is quite similar. Spin casting is intended to incorporate the advantages of both spinning and bait casting. The closed-face spinning reel mounts on top of the rod, like a conventional bait casting reel. The only finger manipulation involved is the pressing down —and holding down—of a thumb lever, to lock the line at the reel while the ten-one-ten casting arc is prescribed, after which the lever is released, to release the line and let the lure fly toward its target in the usual manner.

Slightly different (longer) rods are available for use with spin-casting reels, but you can also use a regular bait casting rod.

There are those who feel that spin casting is the easiest form of casting for the beginner to learn.

Thus far we have considered only how bait casting and spinning tackle can be used for casting. Now let's see how such equipment is used to catch fish.

You will recall that a good bait casting reel will have provision for placing it in "free-spool" condition, to make casting easier, and to eliminate whirling reel handles that might otherwise injure the angler's knuckles while casting. Then, upon completion of the cast, when the reel handle is advanced slightly, the spool becomes engaged once more with the gear chain. Now, should a fish grab the offering, a built-in and adjustable spool brake—or "drag," as it is more commonly referred to—will yield line to the fish only to the extent of the drag adjustment.

Similarly, when the bail of an open-faced spinning reel is pushed to the open (disengaged) position—or the line pickup mechanism of a closed-face spinning reel is disengaged by turning the reel handle backward until it stops—line is able freely to leave the stationary spool during the cast. When the reel handle is advanced, in either case, the bail or other pickup mechanism is activated. An anti-reverse lever can now usually be operated to prevent the reel handle from flying backward to injure the angler's hand when a fish takes out line. In this condition the reel brake, or drag, takes over.

Ideally, the drag adjustment of any reel should be maintained at that critical value where the brake clutch begins to slip, or yield line, to the fish just before the line is apt to break from the pulling pressure. Set the drag too lightly and the fish—if it be a big one—can continue to rob you of line until he takes it all. Adjust the drag too tightly and the resistance being offered by the reel brake, added to the pulling force being exerted by the fish, will exceed the breaking strength of the line—and it will break!

Unfortunately, the reel brake adjustment is not one that can be made once and then forgotten. For the conditions that determine optimum drag can change considerably while a fish is being fought. Consider this example: when a struggling fish is still quite close to the angler the total energy exerted by—or upon—the line will include the pull of the fish, the braking action of the reel drag, and the resistance encountered by the line as it passes over the rod line guides. However, should the fish launch into a long run, and perhaps put a big curve, or belly, in the line when it changes direction—as a fleeing fish often will—this added resistance, resulting from the additional amount of line moving through the water, can cause the line to part!

In other words, the extra energy exerted by the fish to pull the additional amount of line through the water, can build up to a pressure greater than the breaking strength of the line.

And here is another little-understood truth concerning reel drag: tests have revealed that when the diameter of the line on a reel spool melts down to one half its original size, the resistance offered to the outgoing line (i.e., the reel's braking action for a given drag adjustment) may increase *three times,* or more!

Other conditions also apply, further to complicate the drag problem. Bringing one's rod tip up from the horizontal to the fish-fighting position, to put a bend in the rod, can more than double the breaking pressure that is applied to the line.

Constantly changing fishing conditions like these make it impossible for any reel manufacturer to calibrate the drag adjustment in actual pounds of pressure that a given setting will cause to be exerted upon the line. A good rule of thumb to follow, instead, is to use a drag setting no more than one third the breaking strength of the line being used. Then use finger pressure against the spool of a revolving reel, or the outgoing spinning line, as the case may be, to provide what additional drag may prove necessary.

Keep clearly in mind the need for *reducing* drag as a running fish takes out considerable line. (The natural tendency of the amateur fisherman is to do just the opposite; the harder the fish fights, the more drag the angler is tempted to apply at the reel.) Later, after you have succeeded in turning the fish and have reclaimed a safe amount of line, you can increase the pressure at the reel. Proper reel drag adjustment is one of the least understood procedures in the world of fishing.

The beginning fisherman should perform this simple test; it will provide him a very helpful mental picture, to be used under actual fishing conditions later, how much pressure is brought upon the line by various adjustments of the reel drag, by various degrees of finger pressure upon the reel spool, and by different bends in the rod: Secure a small fish-weighing scale (a pull type spring balance). Fasten one side of this scale to some secure object, the opposite side to the end of your line.

Now back away from the scale about twenty yards. Have a companion call out the changing scale readings as you exert a steady pull, first with the rod lowered, and pointing right at the scale; then with the rod bent at 45 degrees, at 90 degrees. Do this for various settings of the reel drag, and with various finger pressures applied against reel spool and line. You may be surprised . . .

Of course, before a fish can be fought it must first be found—and lured into striking some kind of offering. Subsequent chapters will explain how to find fresh water species in streams, rivers and lakes; saltwater fish in bays, inlets and in the ocean. The strike usually results from a fish's hunger—although he may attack from anger, even curiosity, too—and it will also be explained later how this is brought about by still fishing from boat or shore; by wading, casting and trolling.

To battle a fish successfully with bait casting (or trolling) tackle an angler must alternately "pump" and reel; that is, raise the straining rod tip slowly to force the resisting fish toward him, then drop the tip abruptly to reel in quickly the brief amount of slack so gained. This can prove to be a back- and arm-tiring process.

A right-handed angler reels with his right hand. Meanwhile, the other hand holds the bait casting (or trolling) rod, with the fingers wrapped about the upper rod grip. Should the reel have no level-wind mechanism, the thumb and forefinger of the rod hand must play the additional role of guiding the returning line upon the spool, as evenly as possible.

A user of bait casting tackle can suffer a nasty thumb burn, the result of friction heat developed between this finger and a rapidly revolving reel spool, should a fish suddenly break into a strong run and only the thumb is available to slow this dash.

Some bait casters and spin fishermen prefer to fight a fish by holding the rod in both hands, away from the body. Others like to lodge the rod butt against the stomach, sometimes hooking the end beneath the belt to get added pumping leverage.

Many of our game fish are jumpers and it is at such time, particularly, that slack line should be avoided—for a lure that is permitted to swing freely is more apt to become dislodged than one held in position by a steady line pressure. On the other hand, if the line is held too taut when the fish jumps, it may land upon it, causing breakage of a light leader, if one is being used. Many anglers who pursue tarpon, and other big fish, have developed the habit of carefully pushing both arms—and therefore the rod—in the direction of a jumping fish, to compensate for the sudden new pressure created by the jump. This is called "bowing" to the fish.

It is good practice, also, not to crank a spinning reel when a fish is pulling out line. Such cranking will not regain any line (the drag is slipping purposely, remember) and it merely puts troublesome twists into the taut line.

The first rule in landing a fish, whether by net, gaff or by hand—whether wading, or on a shore, or in a boat—is to make certain the fish has become so tired he is ready for landing. If not, you may well lose the prize as it makes a characteristic last-ditch lunge to escape. This can also break your rod tip.

If you are using a landing net, always lead the fish headfirst into the net, on a short, taut line. That way, should the fish become alarmed suddenly at your proximity, he can only plunge deeper into the net. Should the net not be of a size sufficient to engulf the fish safely, a gaff should be used, instead.

Probably the safest way to gaff a fish is to bring the sharp hook quickly upward, into the fish's soft stomach, about midway between head and tail. (See *Photo 30.*) Then, preferably with the same motion, lift the fish from the water.

Should you be without either net or gaff, and the fish is a large one, your only alternative is to try and lead the fish into shallow water, there to beach it. You can then use one hand to grasp the prize in the gills and carry it onto dry ground. (But be careful! A violently thrashing fish on a beach can easily hook you with your own lure . . . and often a club on the head, beforehand, can spare such painful injury.)

Small fish like trout and bass can usually be lifted safely from the water by getting a firm grip in the gills with one hand. To do this slide the fingers in cautiously from the underside, meanwhile keeping the fish's head up with a short line. Try to exert equal hand pressure on both gills.

Black bass can be handled easily by getting a firm grip over the lip of the lower jaw, using the thumb and forefinger to do this. Then press downward, meanwhile lifting the fish from the water in a position to maintain this jaw-paralyzing pressure. Some anglers also disable a fish by pressing inward simultaneously against both eyes as they lift the catch from the water.

In spite of such precautions, it is surprising how much fin and mouth damage even a small fish can inflict upon an angler, when given a chance to do so. So land all fish carefully.

Chapter 11
How to Fly Cast (and Fish)

Fly fishing is regarded by many—including this writer—to be the ultimate angling achievement. It can produce more fish, can prove more interesting and intriguing, than any other kind of fishing. Fly fishing can do this for several reasons. First, flies can provide life-sized, extremely natural-looking replicas of foods that fish prefer. Too, the combination of hand-held line and long, sensitive rod results in what is—for the most part—direct, intimate contact with the struggling fish.

Fly fishing is fun fishing—yet many beginners, unfortunately, never experience this fun. They give up at the outset, overwhelmed, because they fail to use the right approach. Or, worse, they are discouraged from even starting by certain experienced fly casters who seem almost determined to discourage newcomers . . . by offering complicated advice, or by publishing lofty writings, on an otherwise simple subject.

This is too bad. It is sheer nonsense, in fact. I will readily admit that fly fishing can be the final step upward for an angler. But children and grandmothers alike have become effective fly fishermen after but a few intelligent casting lessons.

Briefly, fly fishing involves casting out a weighted line. The line must have weight, since flies—unlike spin and bait casting lures—are practically weightless. Hence, a fly alone could not develop sufficient momentum, when cast out, to pull an ordinary line out, were we to try and use one on a fly reel.

After the fly line has been cast out it must be picked up again from the water (one reason why a fly rod must be quite long). This line pickup is accomplished with a brisk upward motion of the rod tip, to about the vertical position. The angler then waits until the line straightens out above, and behind, his shoulder. The line is then brought forward again, powered by the proper rod movement, and released by one's other hand at the right instant to cause the line to shoot forward, and complete the cast.

That, in essence, is all there is to fly casting. If you can learn but this much, you will have little trouble catching fish with flies. Later, should you wish, you can—after considerable practice—become an expert distance caster (an ability you will seldom use under average fishing conditions) or one able to drop his fly exactly where he wants it, and so on.

Chapter 10 explained how it is the weight of the backward-cast bait or lure that flexes or "loads" the properly balanced bait casting or spinning rod—thereby imparting to the stick the power needed to shoot the lure forward again immediately to its destination. In fly casting it is the weight of the line, instead, that causes the rod to "work" properly, and the need for balanced tackle is even *more* important.

A fly casting outfit can be said to be in proper balance when a *change* in relationship between any of the components involved— that is, the rod, reel, line or the weight, size or shape of the lure— causes *you* to be able to use the outfit less efficiently.

For example, today fly lines are available in weights that vary from sixty to 380 grains (i.e., AFTMA line numbers 1 to 12—refer to the AFTMA table at the end of this chapter). Were you to try and cast each of these twelve fly lines, in turn, using the same rod, reel and lure each time, you would likely discover that only one—perhaps two, under certain conditions—worked best for you. You would find yourself able to cast this line farther, and more easily, than the others. Should you make a change, and substitute one of the other lines for this optimum one, your fly casting would suffer accordingly; your outfit would be unbalanced.

A spin fisherman can make a similar test, by substituting sinkers of different weights at the end of his line. He will discover that there is one weight that he can cast farther, and more easily, than the others. He may be tempted to increase this weight, to cast farther, but he will find his casting distance decreasing, instead. Reason: the "action"— or degree of shaft taper, or stiffness—of the rod is such that the shaft cannot flex, or load up with power, to full advantage while trying to accommodate this additional weight.

The manufacturers of fly rods, particularly, are aware of this. As a result, nearly always they will mark their product with the number of the fly line which the American Fishing Tackle Manufacturers

Association has found will work best with the particular type of rod involved. This AFTMA recommended weight information is not always completely accurate; you may still have to experiment somewhat to achieve perfect tackle balance. But it sure does decrease considerably the need for such experimentation.

Not to be outdone, some line manufacturers, in turn, recommend which of their lines should be used with rods of various length and action. The table which follows is a general guide provided by the Cortland Line Company; it is intended to help balance fly rods of various lengths and actions to floating fly lines made by this company. A fly line may be manufactured to float—in which case it will carry the designation F, along with its weight and taper information—or it may be designed to sink (S). Some lines are of the same diameter throughout their length (designated L, to indicate such a level line). Others are purposely made to bulge in the center portion, then taper off at each end. (Such a double taper is indicated by the box marking DT.) And some lines have their greatest diameter—hence casting weight—at the forward end (WF, for weight-forward). These various line profiles are shown in *Figure 11-1*.

The Cortland Company is quick to point out that this is only a very general guide to "probable" balance between fly rod and proper line weight, and urges further checking, where necessary.

A floating line must be used to fish dry flies and bugs, since these lures are intended to float. A sinking line is necessary to carry streamers, and other wet flies, beneath the surface. (Nymph fishing, for instance, is nearly always bottom fishing.)

The level line is the least expensive and is used most often for casting wet flies and live bait. A double taper is intended primarily for dry fly fishing, since the taper makes it possible to cast these delicate lures with the gentleness that is required. A "bug" or other weight-forward line (the "rocket" taper, in the case of Cortland-made fly lines) has its heaviest portion closest to the leader and hook, thereby making possible long casts, when these are needed. This WF feature permits the casting of bass bugs, and other large— hence wind-resistant—lures, when another line might fail. Too, the WF line becomes almost a must for saltwater flymen, since these anglers are nearly always subject to stronger breezes in exposed estuarine areas, and out upon the open sea.

Until the late 1950s practically all fly lines were made of silk. This made it possible to use letters of the alphabet to designate the

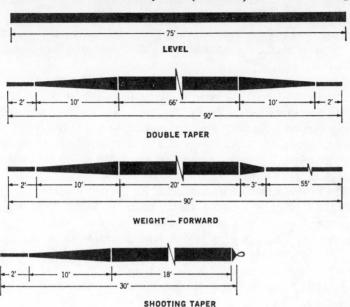

Figure 11–1 Diagrams of the Four Types of Typical Fly Lines (Courtesy of Scientific Anglers, Midland, Mich.)

Length and Weight of Rod	Level Line	Double Taper Line	Rocket Taper Line	Bug Taper Line
7 ft. Light Action	L5F	DT5F	WF5F	—
7½ or 8 ft. Light Action	L5F	DT5F	WF5F	—
8 ft. Medium Action	L6F	DT6F	WF6F	—
8½ ft. Light Action	L6F	DT6F	WF6F	—
8½ ft. Med. Action	L7F	DT7F	WF7F	WF8F
8½ ft. Heavy Action	L9F	DT9F	WF9F	WF9F
9 ft. Light Action	L7F	DT7F	WF7F	WF8F
9 ft. Medium Action	L8F	DT8F	WF8F	WF8F
9 ft. Heavy Action	L9F	DT9F	WF9F	WF9F
9½ ft. Medium Action	L9F	DT9F	WF9F	WF9F

various tapers, which were similar to those in use today. When today's lines of synthetic materials appeared, however, a new system had to be devised. For, whereas previously a certain alphabet letter would serve to indicate a definite line diameter, regardless who was the manufacturer (they were all using silk, remember), now mass confusion reigned: the new materials (nylon and Dacron) did not weigh the same as silk for a given diameter! Hence these new lines cast quite differently.

The line manufacturers agreed to forget the old alphabet method (as you should, too). Henceforth, it would be the weight, in grains, of the first thirty feet of the fly line that would serve as a reference. From then on a No. 6 fly line, for example, would always weigh 160 grains, regardless whether it was a floater or a sinker, or level, double-tapered or forward-tapered. A No. 9 line would always weigh 240 grains in all these designs; and so on. Amen.

The fly reel must also be considered for the part it plays in making possible a properly balanced casting outfit. For most fly fishing the reel serves simply as a storage space for the line. And, since most anglers cast out only thirty feet of line, or less, while fly fishing (a fact that is probably quite contrary to what you have been led to believe), this permits use of a relatively simple fly reel, either the direct drive (reel handle operated) or automatic type, as was described in Chapter 1.

Nevertheless, the reel should also effectively counterbalance the weight of the rod. This is necessary to insure maximum casting ease and therefore the least tiring of the angler's arm. The physical balance of a fully rigged fly rod should take place at a point at, or slightly in front of, the cork handgrip. To determine where this point is located, balance the rod atop a board fence, or similar narrow surface. If necessary, use a heavier, or lighter, reel.

Fly reels for big game fishing sport will weigh considerably more than the usual simple, single-action reel. Sturdier construction is the keynote in the big game reels, which also employ powerful drag mechanisms that add weight. But then these reels are used with considerably heavier rods, too, and this helps maintain the physical balance needed for the easiest casting.

Finally, the lure, too, can play its own important role in determining the dynamic balance of a fly rod outfit. It is true that the weight and wind resistance of a dry fly may be considered negligible. But cast a big bug, or a streamer—on a windy day, especially—and that can be something else! Under such circumstances the flyman must use a heavy weight-forward line. And this heavy line, in turn, automatically calls for a correspondingly heavier rod, to balance the line. And the large fly started all this . . .

To cast a fly properly, be it large or small, a correctly tapered leader must be used. A good cast demands that the fly line loop must "turn over" (i.e., straighten out) correctly at the conclusion of the forward cast. Considerable energy is imparted to the leader when this takes place. (The end of the fly line may be traveling several hundred miles per hour!) A correctly tapered leader will reduce this energy to a value suitable for depositing the fly lightly upon the water, with a minimum of fish-scaring splash. The action of the tapered leader can be compared to the use of three garden hoses, of diameters 1, ¾ and ½ inches, connected together to cause a reduction of water pressure. The force of water emerging from the tip of the half-inch hose will be noticeably less than it was at the one-inch faucet, for a given opening.

The leader will vary from about six to fourteen feet, depending upon specific fishing conditions (to be discussed in detail in later chapters). It will decrease either smoothly or noticeably in diameter, depending upon whether the leader is the manufactured or self-tied type, respectively. The "butt," or area of largest cross section, is positioned closest to the fly line, and should not be less than about two thirds the fly line diameter, for best results.

A typical angler-tied leader might consist of lengths of 30, 20 and 12 pound monofilament. The 30 pound mono will comprise about two thirds of the leader length. (Some flycasters prefer a butt section of so-called stiff nylon, the remainder of the leader being made of the softer, more pliable mono. It is believed that this provides for greater casting ease.) Each section of this three-part leader should be fastened to the next with a blood knot. The 30 pound butt will be joined to the fly line with a nail, or a needle, knot.

The leader should be of sufficient length—and limber enough—to avoid scaring the fish either by the splash of the landing fly line, or by the fish becoming aware of the presence of the heavier line. The last is of special importance when the water is very clear. The leader should also permit proper retrieve action for the fly; and not "overpower" the lure. A delicate fly obviously requires a fine diameter leader end, or "tippet" as it is called: perhaps one of only 4 pound breaking strength, maybe even less. This prevents the fly from being jerked unceremoniously through the water. Or, equally annoying, pulled bottomward by the too heavy leader.

Tapered leaders can be purchased. Lengths of 7½, 9 and 12 feet are standard, and a wide variety of diameters are available.

A good beginner's balanced fly casting outfit can be assembled around an 8- or 8½-foot rod of medium-stiff action. So let's see how such tackle can be used to cast properly.

Select a single-action (1:1 ratio) fly reel of a size and weight that will both adequately store the fly line and counterbalance the rod. Wind a fly line of correct weight and taper onto the spool of this reel (I would suggest a WF line for easier casting), after first securing the end of the fly line with the knot described in Chapter 2.

This particular rod will probably work best with a No. 6 or a No. 7 line. If, after testing, we find we can use the heavier one, the No. 7, we will use it—since a somewhat heavier line is generally easier for a beginner to cast.

Mount the reel. Note that it goes at the very end of the long rod, unlike a spinning or bait casting reel. The reel mounts on the underside of the rod, too. If you are a right-hand caster, the reel should be mounted so the handles are on the right, and vice versa.

Pull some fly line from the reel, about a dozen feet. Pass the end of this line through all the rod guides, so that it extends about six feet beyond the tip. Fly line is supple and has the annoying habit of slipping from one's hand—immediately to drop downward, and back through, every guide on the long rod. To avoid this, first double the end of the line, for a foot or so. Then push this doubled end through the guides as you string the rod. This way, should the line slip from your fingers, it will remain in position.

The Overhead Fly Cast

We will learn to cast on land (although you can also use water). So select a clear section of lawn, parking lot, recreation area, etc. Place the rod on the ground and pull about thirty feet of line from the reel. Stretch this line in a straight line before the rod, on the ground. We will not use a leader, or a fly, on the line.

Now pick up the rod, so that the fingers of what is to be your casting hand are wrapped comfortably about the cork grip, with the thumb on top. Picture yourself standing before a large clock face, and raise the rod tip slowly from horizontal to the nine-thirty or ten o'clock position (see *Figure 11–2*). This should remove all slack from the line—something that is *important*, before you can properly commence either a backward or forward cast.

Should there still be some slack in the line, remove this by reaching

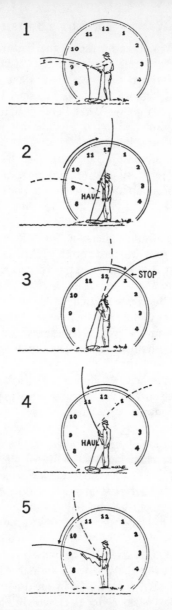

Figure 11–2 How to Fly Cast: (1) Tension for pickup—Slight line pull, slight rod lift, (2) Pickup and haul—First haul, (3) Back cast and pause —W-A-I-T until line reaches rearmost limit, (4) Forward cast and haul— Second haul, (5) "Shooting" the line—Release the extra line for maximum distance (Courtesy of Weber Tackle Co., Stevens Point, Wisc.)

up to the first line guide and grasping the line there between thumb and forefinger of what will henceforth be referred to as your line hand. Pull down through the rod guides whatever amount of line may be necessary to remove the slack. Let such line hang down in a loop, below the reel. (I go into detail here, since this will also be your preparation procedure, prior to lifting line from the water to cast, later, while you are actually fishing.)

At this stage, before casting, the line must be anchored—to prevent it from slipping from the reel, to move upward through the rod guides as you bring up the rod to casting position. This anchoring can be done in two ways: (1) hold the line taut with your line hand, or (2) transfer the line to the fingers of your rod hand, using these to clamp it against the underside of the rod grip.

Now, with the rod arm comfortably close to the body, elbow pointing downward, raise the forearm (hence the rod) quickly to about the one o'clock position. This is done by keeping the wrist rigid, allowing only the elbow to bend.

This upward snap of the rod will cause the entire fly line to be picked up smartly from the ground. The line will go sailing backward, high over your right shoulder, in the form of a big, open-ended loop, as shown.

(And you had better keep that loop *high*. It will collapse awkwardly to earth, instead, if you (1) failed to raise the forearm and rod with sufficient snap and power; or (2) relaxed your wrist and allowed the rod tip to travel too far backward; or (3) if you waited too long to start the forward portion of the cast, which will be described next.)

Without otherwise changing body position, glance back over your rod shoulder. Watch the loop unfold and straighten out from its own momentum. Feel the slight tug at the rod tip that comes when the line is completely straightened behind you. (Normally, while fishing, you would not be looking back, and this tug would be your only indication.)

The *instant* the line is straight you must begin the forward cast. This is done by driving the rod (i.e., with the still rigid wrist and forearm) forward—*not downward*—in an arc that carries the rod tip from one o'clock back to about eleven o'clock, as shown in the illustration. This forward thrust imparts the power necessary to shoot the line away straight before you, toward its destination. The action involved here is similar to that of hammering a nail into a wall before you.

Finally, the rod tip is allowed to follow through, and drop downward to—or near—the horizontal position as the fly line now stretches out to full length and drops to earth (water).

That's all there is to it. Practice it again and again: up and back, pause, forward . . . up and back, pause, forward . . . etc.

Had we been fishing, instead of practicing, the rod would have been pointed toward some specific target during the initial part of the cast, as we drew the line taut in preparation for the upsweeping of the nearly horizontal rod. Then, during the forward cast, we would have aimed at an imaginary spot two or three feet above the target. As we observed the second, or forward, portion of the cast nearing completion—as we saw the forward-sailing loop begin to unfold in the line, or "turn over"—we would have raised the rod tip about a foot. (It will also help if you draw back your casting arm about a foot at this point.)

This causes the fly and leader to strike the surface first, thereby creating the least possible fish-disturbing commotion. (The fly line, meanwhile, has straightened out in midair, after which it falls lightly to the water, instead of plunging into the surface.)

False Casting and Shooting Line

When the flyman repeats a back cast, after making a forward cast, he is said to be "false" casting. False casts are made to enable the angler to judge better the distance to a target site. They can also be used to dry off a fly, by keeping it in motion. False casting is done mainly, however, to increase casting distance—by first getting more line into the air. When sufficient line has been worked out thus, it is allowed to "shoot" out through the rod guides—toward the target—on the final cast. More, shortly, on how to shoot line.

If your fly casting outfit is properly balanced, and if you have learned the necessary rhythm—a backward and forward rod movement that is neither too fast nor too slow—you should be able to keep the fly line in the air with little effort while you complete the necessary number of false casts. This is so because such proper casting might be likened to a smoothly performing power system, suspended in midair, and connected to earth (the angler) for the continuing source of energy needed to overcome losses caused by air resistance, gravity pull and friction. (The last loss takes place mainly at the rod's line guides.)

Theoretically, a mechanical fulcrum, or lever, could be used to replace the angler's casting arm as a source of power, and the balanced system could be expected to operate indefinitely. (Actually, however, the human ability is required to compensate for additional energy required by changing wind and other varying conditions.)

To practice false casting we shall put about thirty feet of fly line into the air, as before. This time, however, we shall not begin with that amount of line stretched out upon the earth before us. Instead, with perhaps only a yard, or so, of line extending beyond the rod tip, use the thumb and forefinger of the line hand to strip (pull) about six additional feet from the reel. Hold this line comfortably with the line hand, hanging down from the fingers in loops a foot or so in length.

Bring the rod quickly back to the one o'clock position, then forward to eleven o'clock—the motion used previously for casting practice. On the forward portion, let go the line, allowing the loops to straighten out and be pulled upward through the rod guides, to become airborne. Without allowing the line to settle to earth, make a back cast. While you are doing this strip off an additional amount of line from the reel, holding the coils in the line hand, as before. Release this in the same way, during the following forward cast.

You are false casting. Do this until you have enough line in the air to reach your target area. Then complete the cast.

By this time you have learned enough about casting—back and forward casts, and how to keep line in the air—to go fishing. Before we discuss some additional casts that flymen use, let's consider any troubles you may have encountered thus far.

Is your line falling to earth behind you, before you can bring it forward again? (A common fault with beginners.) Correct this by reminding yourself that you must bring the line *up*—not merely back—on the back cast. Keep it high. Also, stop applying power to the back cast (i.e., the rod) when the rod is about at the vertical position—and in no case farther back than the one o'clock angle.

Does your fly line pile up in an awkward mess at the end of the forward cast, instead of straightening out fully, as it should? Correct this by not releasing line too soon on the forward cast (i.e., by not shooting line too soon: only after you have stopped the rod at the eleven o'clock forward position—or perhaps a little beyond that— should you release the line held in your line hand).

Are you becoming impatient with yourself? Discouraged? You are likely tiring. Don't try to learn it all at once! A few minutes—perhaps only fifteen, surely not more than thirty—spent at about the same time each day, is a good way to practice.

The Double-Haul Cast

There may be times when the flyman must deliver more than the usual amount of casting power to his rod: perhaps to drive a lure into the wind, or to reach a far-ranging, wary fish on some shoal. The double-haul may then be used to make the rod store more energy; to flex more than usual, and work harder.

Here is the way the double-haul is executed: strip off a considerable amount of line from the reel, and let this fall in coils at your feet. Put as much of this line as you can into the air, by false casting in the usual manner.

Now, as you start still another back cast, grip the line at the first line guide, between thumb and forefinger of the line hand. Pull this line sharply downward, and backward—far as you can reach below and behind you—from the first guide position.

This does two things: it causes the rod to load (bend) more than it normally would. And it forces the fly line to move backward through the air with added speed.

Look over your shoulder as you do this. Watch the rearward-sailing loop. This time, just before the line straightens out fully, release the line. Let it shoot backward an additional distance.

This is done by letting the line leap upward from the coils at your feet, passing through the now circle-forming first two fingers of your line hand as it does this. The line hand, meanwhile, also moves upward, across the chest, and positions itself in readiness near the first line guide.

When you feel that you have shot enough line rearward (you can only shoot so much at a time, else gravity overcomes velocity, and the line falls to the ground) the thumb and forefinger of the line hand are used to stop the outgoing line. This should cause you to feel the telltale tug at the rod tip, indicating that the line has straightened out behind you. At that same moment begin the forward cast, in the usual manner.

Now, just as the forward cast is nearly completed, line is stripped sharply downward and backward again—far as you can reach. Once again the rod is accordingly made to flex more, to work harder, than usual. And once more line flies forward faster than it ordinarily would.

Finally, as the rod is allowed to follow through, to drop down toward the horizontal (i.e., to about nine-thirty o'clock), the line is released for the last time. This allows additional coils to leap upward and out through the guides. The double-haul cast has been completed.

(Should still more distance have been required, the action would have been repeated, instead of allowing the line to fall to the water on the forward cast. The actual distance achieved depends upon the flycaster's physical ability and sense of timing. When making this powerful cast every part of the body seems to join in—arms, head, back, legs merge in a sort of rock-and-roll movement—the object being to impart every bit of energy humanly possible to the whistling line, yet without losing the vital timing.)

The Roll Cast

This one involves no back cast. It is used when growths or other obstructions behind the angler prohibit a back cast. To roll cast you simply "roll a hoop" in a direction away from your casting position. The out-moving line becomes the hoop.

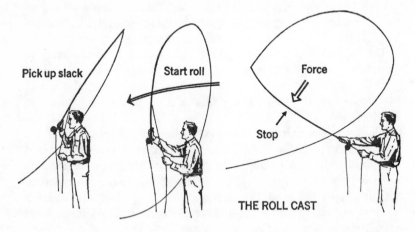

Figure 11-3

Figure 11-3 shows the movements of the roll cast. Twitch the rod tip, or use some other means, to get a few yards of line out onto the water before you. (In extreme cases you may even be obliged to throw out a handful of line coils to accomplish this.) Next, strip from the reel an adequate additional amount of line, for shooting purpose, allowing this to fall at your feet. Then raise the rod carefully, drawing the floating line toward you (i.e., straightening it on the water) as you bring the rod back past your rod hand shoulder to about the one o'clock position. The rod should be tipped outward at about a 45-degree angle from this shoulder, to avoid hooking yourself with the fly when you make the roll cast.

At this stage some of the line should be hanging down a few feet behind you, extending from rod tip to water, with the remainder of the line in the water.

Now complete the cast simply by pushing the rod suddenly forward and downward. This should cause all the line to zip free of the water and "roll" forward through the air. (There may be times when it does not escape the water completely, and is shortened in its forward movement accordingly.)

If you have put enough energy into the forward push of the rod, you will find that the line is moving with sufficient speed to pull with it—i.e., to "shoot" outward—quite a bit, if not all, the line waiting at your feet.

One of the first requirements to make a fish strike a fly is not to frighten the quarry off during presentation of the lure. We have already stated that a sloppy cast can do this; a noisy pileup of the heavy fly line, instead of the proper gentle descent of the light lure and leader. Another way to frighten fish is to cast beyond them. So work the nearest water first, gradually reaching outward with your casts. And if you see a fish rise to feed, don't cast into the center of the widening ring of ripples. You will do better by casting to one side.

Of course, you will not drop your fly even close to such a rise if you've not practiced casting accuracy beforehand. You can do this in much the same manner that was discussed for the bait and spin casters in Chapter 10; by using a newspaper, or other target, on a lawn, etc. Don't try too hard. A few minutes daily will achieve more than long, tiring workouts. The outgoing line is stopped at the proper distance simply by applying pressure from the fingers of the line hand, to prevent further movement of line through the rod's line guides.

At this point, were we fishing instead of practicing, some additional hand movements would be involved. This is, after the moving lure had been slowed, then stopped altogether (by the line hand, *before* the lure has opportunity to fall to the surface) we would shift control of the line from the line hand to the rod hand. This is done by clamping the line against the underside of the rod, using the fingers of the rod-holding hand for this purpose. It is done to free the line hand for stripping in line, thereby imparting fish-attracting movement to the fly. The pressure from the rod hand fingers, meanwhile, prevents the retrieved line from slipping up and out through the line guides (i.e., pulled either by its own weight, beyond the tip, or by a fish, should one be on).

The fly can be moved through the water either by stripping in line with pulls of varying length and speed, or by twitching the rod tip, or by a combination of both movements. Don't move the rod tip very far upward in your effort to impart lure action. Keep the tip pointed toward the lure. Remember, you are using a limber rod. You will need all the upswing possible to set the hook, so don't place yourself out of position at the start.

The line hand, too, aids with the hook setting, of course. In fact, many anglers use this hand mainly for striking. The stripping hand should always operate *below* the rod hand, to make sure that the line is always under control, should a strike come. That is, with the method I am describing, line is pulled through the partly relaxed fingers of the rod hand, each time that a strip is made. Hence, those fingers are able immediately to clamp the line tightly against the rod, in the event of a strike. The rod can then be brought sharply upward, and backward, to aid further in setting the hook.

Were the angler briefly to surrender control of the line each time a strip is made—as some fishermen unthinkingly do—by reaching above the rod hand to make a new pull, then transferring this line to the fingers of the rod hand for holding, a strike is apt to come at that very moment. For fish have a habit of following a moving lure, then striking when the lure pauses before them—as it will each time at the conclusion of a strip, or pull, on the line.

Some flymen allow the line to fall in coils at their feet as they pull it in (or float upon the surface, should they be wading). Others prefer to store the line in the palm of their line hand as they retrieve. This last can be accomplished by using a wrist motion to turn the palm alternately upward and downward, each time taking a new "bite" of the line (i.e., adding a new fold of the line to those small folds already held in the palm).

A fish that strikes hard usually manages to hook itself. However, there are times when the offering may be accepted gingerly, and rejected immediately, should not all appear normal. It is then that the angler must be able to set the hook himself, quickly and effectively, before the offering can be rejected.

This is done best, of course, if the fish can be observed approaching the bait in clear, shallow water. Or, even better, on the surface. The angler can then co-ordinate both what he sees and feels, to bury the barb in the fish's mouth at precisely the right moment.

When you are fishing "blind," however, it is not nearly so easy. Then it becomes especially important that you maintain a taut line during the retrieve: else you likely will not feel the first telltale "touch" against the lure. (This is one reason why I grow weary reading about those super flymen who must invariably cast super distances to take their fish. How do they know when to set the hook? With all that line out . . . it seems that 100 feet has to be the minimum, if one is to be classed with these experts . . . and a fly rod being the limber instrument it is, it strikes me that even an unhurried fish could tie a knot in the angler's leader without the super flycaster becoming aware of it!)

In anticipation of the strike, the rod should be pointing in the direction of the lure: low, and nearly horizontal. When the retrieve is made it should be varied: perhaps several even six-inch pulls on the line at the outset, this followed by several longer strips—maybe two or three feet of line pulled in each time—these strips being angled sharply downward, and backward, with a single sweeping motion of the line hand. The rod tip can be moved simultaneously, also, if you wish: short up-and-down swings of the tip. This will add to the fly's tantalizing movement through the water, causing it to dart and dive and twist even more—hopefully resembling a helpless bait fish as it does this.

It is important to point out that we will be wasting our time—even with this appealing movement of the lure—if we fail first to get the fly down to where the fish are. The depth at which the lure is made to operate will depend upon the current (if any) that may be present, the speed of the retrieve, and the "sink rate" of the fly itself. That is, the larger the hook that is used, the heavier the fly will be, and the more quickly the lure will sink. Hence to get a fly down to the proper depth on a bonefish flat, for example, you may find it necessary to switch from a fly dressed on a No. 6 hook to one using a No. 4, perhaps even a No. 2.

The strike will usually come at the end of a strip or—if the retrieve is being made across a current—when the current swings the fly to the end of its drift. When you feel the strike, raise the nearly horizontal rod sharply to the 45-degree "fighting" angle. At the same time, aid this initial hook-setting movement with a single long and hard inward strip (pulling the line perhaps as much as three feet, if you have long arms) by the line hand.

Once the fish is hung, line will go racing upward, and outward, through the line guides of the already bending rod. And it will be your next responsibility to make sure the coils of fly line leaping upward from the vicinity of your feet do not become entangled en route—either around your feet, or perhaps around something lying in the bottom of the boat (if you are using a boat), or anything else that may obstruct and snag. If the line does manage to bunch up and create a blockage at the first line guide, that guide—and perhaps several others, if not *all* of them—may be torn away, and the rod tip broken, too—should it be a really big fish you have hooked!

So let the outgoing line run first through the smoothing fingers of your line hand—this hand being held purposely high, and away from the rod. That way, should you feel a knot, you can likely clamp the outgoing line temporarily beneath the fingers of the rod hand while you safely free the tangle.

Once you get the last of the previously stripped-in line thus safely back on the reel, you can proceed to breathe somewhat easier as you battle the fish "off the reel," as they say. Let him run. The more he expends energy, the more tired he will become. And the sooner he will be ready for netting or gaffing or beaching.

Keep in mind the need for *reducing* drag as the fish continues to pull off more line. This can be done by decreasing the reel's brake tension—should the reel boast a brake—or by applying less finger pressure to the spinning spool flange, or by a combination of both these methods, as may be required.

When the fish has shown unmistakable signs of tiring, when it is no longer so "green" it might endanger your tackle if brought in close, you can lead it—held now on a short line—headfirst into a landing net of adequate size. Preferably, the net should be held by a fishing companion. Or, should the fish be too large for netting, use a gaff—or beach it—as was discussed in Chapter 10.

There is, of course, more to fly fishing than what I have included here. It is quite possible, for instance, that you may develop annoying so-called "wind knots" in your leader when you set out to fly-fish. You may, in fact, even snap off the fly from the end of the leader, so great is the pressure that can be built up during a back cast. But what you have been told in this chapter should get you started quite nicely as a fly fisherman, if you follow directions. The rest will follow naturally, as you experiment and compare notes with other flycasters.

You can, for example, avoid wind knots (these are actual over-hand knots that appear in the leader; very aggravating) by simply not tipping the rod forward until the *conclusion* of a properly made forward cast (that is, cast with the rod held at the one o'clock angle as it is pushed forward). Again, to avoid snapping off your fly you need only use sufficient force on the back cast to straighten out the line fully—and make certain you wait until it *has* straightened out before beginning the forward cast.

In conclusion, while it is true that today's floating fly lines have built-in flotation, do not confuse the one-time need for greasing a line (to make it float) with the still present need for cleaning your line. A fly line has a tendency to pick up a coating of mud and slime that can reduce its suppleness, and therefore the ease with which it may be cast. So clean your line as the need arises. The manufacturer usually provides a small can of cleaner at the time of purchase. If not, cleaner can be purchased separately. After cleaning, wipe off any excess with a cloth, to avoid gumming of the rod guides.

AFTMA Fly Line Standards

Line No.	Weight in Grains	Line No.	Weight in Grains
1	60	7	185
2	80	8	210
3	100	9	240
4	120	10	280
5	140	11	330
6	160	12	380

Chapter 12
Stream and River Fishing

Observe an experienced angler as he fishes a stream or river. You will see him carefully probing certain stretches of water with his casts. Chances are that he will pass up the remainder of the shoreline with hardly a second glance.

This man is wisely concerning himself only with the most promising water: those areas that offer the three main conditions necessary for angling success: fish food, safety and comfort—in that order. He may not encounter all three of these at once, for that is the ideal fishing situation. Meanwhile, our searching angler continues to "think like a fish." As he surveys the water before him he asks himself, "Were I a fish, where would I swim here to find food, safety and comfort?"

Even should but two of the three important conditions exist, and one of these is food, the angler can still enjoy good fishing.

Natural food for fish was discussed in detail in Chapter 3.

Safety conditions exist when a fish can enjoy protection from some predator—usually some other, and larger, fish—that would otherwise be able to inflict harm. Perhaps there is a tiny pocket of dense grass or roots into which a fleeing school of minnows can dart to escape a pursuing muskellunge or northern pike. Or some small hole beneath a submerged stump, maybe a rocky crevice, inside which a terrified panfish can hover in safety while a frustrated bigmouth bass fins back and forth close outside, glaring its impatience.

A mat of floating grass, or a bed of lily pads, can safely hide a basking walleye from the beady glance of a hungry fish hawk circling overhead. And farther back in these same grassy shallows, where the water is perhaps but an inch or two in depth, a newly hatched group of baby fish, maybe still only tadpole-size, can enjoy a measure of safety while their mother forages for food elsewhere. Were the water not so shallow there, these fry would be quickly eaten by some adult fish—sometimes their own parent!

As for comfort, most fish become uncomfortable—just like humans—when the weather becomes too hot, or too cold. Most species feed best when the water temperature ranges between 50 and 60 degrees Fahrenheit. To enjoy this temperature range, or "comfort zone," fish move about considerably, as we shall see in the next chapter. A black bass, for instance, will seek the warmth of shoreline shallows after dark—yet desert such an area during the noonday heat, seeking then the cooler depths, instead.

There are other conditions, too, that affect a fish's comfort. A strong current, for example, can prove tiring. So fish will seek the quiet water behind rocks and other bottom obstructions. Here, too, they can also lie hidden, waiting to dart out upon passing small fish, or other food. A bottom obstruction, therefore, can provide two of the three main ingredients necessary for top fishing: food and comfort. The wise angler knows this, and places his casts accordingly.

Chapters 3 and 4 explained in detail how natural and artificial baits can be used for fishing. Steady water movement (current) is more apt to be present in a stream or river than in a lake or bay, and this truth can be used to advantage when presenting a bait or lure. Minnows, worms and other baits—small spoons, spinners and swimming plugs used with a spinning outfit—or wet flies and nymphs— can all be cast upstream. The current is then allowed to carry the offering downstream, making it tumble and turn invitingly en route —hopefully in a manner to attract a watching trout, bass or other game fish. Once such a "drift" has been completed, and you feel the pull of the current against your now taut line, you must now impart your own action to the lure as you proceed to reel it in.

In some of the deeper streams and rivers you may have to find at what level the fish are feeding or resting. This is done with exploratory casts, first bumping a lure or bait along the bottom, next time allowing it not to sink quite so far before the retrieve is begun, and so on. Sinkers may prove necessary—even with wet flies.

As he follows a stream or riverbank the knowledgeable fisherman keeps clearly in mind the food-carrying role that a current can play. The mouth of a connecting—usually smaller—stream, for instance, would warrant a few exploring casts. Reason: trout and other game fish like to lie in wait at such stream mouths—waiting for insects and other tidbits to be carried to them. The smaller stream very likely is overgrown with bank bushes. And, should a caterpillar fall, or be blown, into the water, it will be carried downstream to the fish waiting at the mouth.

The wise angler approaches such a stream mouth cautiously. He may even come ashore some distance away, should he be wading the main stream or river. For fish have good vision, and can readily see you. This is especially true if they are in shallow, clear water. Fish have good hearing, also. You can easily scare off a trout, for instance, by wading carelessly, by letting your feet strike the bottom hard, by scuffing against rocks, etc. In fact, a trout will spook under such conditions even if you remain completely hidden from view! So make it a practice to approach a pool or other likely fish site only as close as is necessary to make a successful cast. Meanwhile, hold your rod and body profile low as possible against the sky—particularly should you be backlighted by a rising or setting sun.

Keeping in mind how a current can carry food to fish, you should also look for sudden changes in bottom contours—or drop-offs, as these places are called. Reason: the abrupt change in depth at these holes, trenches, etc., causes the current to slow down there considerably. Nymphs and other food being swept helplessly downstream will settle into these drop-offs. Such delay may only be temporary—until the food edges its way out into the current once more, to be carried on its way. But this gives a waiting fish opportunity to pounce upon the offering.

When casting to a drop-off you should do so in such a manner that the lure has time to get down to the level where the fish are waiting. If not, the current will simply sweep your offering past overhead—where the fish either may not see it, or may not feel inclined to chase after it. So place your cast far enough upstream to give your wet fly or nymph sufficient time to sink down. Fortunately, fish always face upstream, so they should be able to see it coming.

Another good place to cast in a stream or river is where a large boulder, perhaps a driftwood jam or an island, causes the current to divide as it encounters the obstruction. This water division can create several good fishing conditions, both at the upstream and downstream (lee) edges of the barrier.

Immediately in the lee, there will exist turbulence where the two currents come together again. This water action often scoops out a bottom hole into which can tumble food being washed downstream. Game fish are therefore attracted to this food basket. The larger fish are also drawn because the strong currents in the lee of the obstruction can greatly hinder the swimming ability of minnows, etc. These natural foods can be rendered quite helpless, in fact.

Then, too, a bit farther on, the action of the rejoining currents is such as to cancel one another somewhat. There will likely be a short stretch of shoal water there. Also, there may be a deposit of the sand, mud and gravel that the currents have washed away to leave a hole immediately in the lee of the boulder or other barrier. In any event, the water can be relatively quiet there; a place where fish can rest as they wait to feed. Hence, here again, the angler finds himself blessed with two of the ideal three fishing conditions: namely, in this particular case, food and comfort. The fisherman should approach from the downstream side (ideally) and cast to a spot just upstream from where the split currents come together again.

The water can be comparatively quiet, or "easy," on the upstream edge of the obstruction, also, as the stream or river current encounters the barrier and tends to "bounce off." Fish could very well be resting in this quieter water, also.

The prudent angler pays close attention to turns and bends as he encounters these along the stream or river shore. At each bend there will exist two different current conditions. At the outer edge of the bend, that is, at the shore which the current strikes the hardest, the water will have cut a channel. Here the depth will be noticeably greater. And here, also, the current tends to deposit insects and other food that floats downstream. In fact, the current likely will have undercut the bank, thereby providing both a cool (shaded) and safe hiding place for fish during daylight hours. If so, the angler could this time find himself happily in the presence of all three of the major fish-catching conditions: food, comfort and safety.

It is this outside, or deeper, part of the bend that offers the best fishing conditions. However, the approaching angler should not overlook the possibility of finding fish resting in the shallower, and quieter, water of the inside bend, also. He should use extra caution in fishing this shallow area, which usually extends outward some distance from shore, for reasons already explained (i.e., the fish will be in a position both to see and to hear him readily).

Trout, especially, like well-aerated water. The pool into which a waterfall tumbles is a good place to find water thus abundantly charged with the plentiful oxygen that trout prefer. However, don't expect to find the fish directly under the falls. Instead, look for them at the edges of the white water—and immediately downstream from the froth and spume created by the turbulence.

Sometimes, it is true, trout will lie deep in such a pool. (Perhaps the fish find a measure of security among the bottom shadows resulting from the patches of foam floating overhead.) More often, however, trout will be found resting in the lees of the downstream rocks and rubble that cause riffles and rapids. Also, in the smoother sections, or "glides," between falls and rapids trout are prone to linger.

Walleyes, smallmouth black bass, and certain other stream and river fish, on the other hand, are prone to avoid the shallower areas. Unlike the trout, these fish prefer the deeper pools and eddies. You may find it necessary to use a small weight to get your bait or lure down to the needed depth.

A beaver dam, brush or timber pileup, or similar obstruction over which a waterway must tumble will also create well-aerated water— both at the dam site and for some distance downstream—hence will attract trout and other fish. These fish may be present, in addition, because the pool created by the falling water offers cool depths—and, very likely, food of some kind, also. And, of course, fish swimming upstream cannot get past such a barrier, and therefore may be lingering in the vicinity.

It is the pools in a stream or river that usually offer the fisherman his best opportunity. This is particularly true should the angler be wading. (Refer to Chapter 7.) Not every pool is ideal, it must be admitted. But it is only the inexperienced angler who passes up one of these potential fish "motels."

The ideal pool site will have a tumbling falls to aerate the water well. There will be present a big rock or two—perhaps, instead, a large fallen tree laying partway across the waterway, just downstream from the falls. This will set up a food-holding, hence fish-attracting eddy current. This rotating current will be in addition to the main one that shoots out of the pool, on the opposite side from the eddy. Once the main current races past the obstruction that has caused the eddy, this main current will slow down into a restful (by comparison), hence fish-inviting, slick or "glide" in the gravel shallows at the "tail" end of the pool area.

You should take your time and cast, in turn, to each promising area of such an ideal pool. Start with the tail of the pool first—for if fish are present they will be most apt to see you, and flush from these shallows. After working the tail out thoroughly with your casts, move upstream, probing the main current, and the back eddy, with additional careful casts. Finally, try a cast or two right into the falls, letting the weight of the tumbling water carry your bait or lure down with it into the pool—as it might a drifting insect, or other bit of natural food. (You may require a small weight to get to the bottom.) If temperature conditions are such that fish are laying at the bottom of the pool, to keep cool or warm, as the case may be, they could be tempted to strike your offering.

It is well to keep in mind that trout avoid warm water—since it lacks sufficient oxygen to keep them comfortable—hence you will find trout in bubbling pools and swift, "splashy" runs and shallow riffles. Another good place to look for trout is at the mouth of a feeder stream that is fed by a spring. The outflowing cold water attracts the trout since it provides them greater temperature comfort, as will, also, an underwater spring in the main waterway.

So don't hesitate to probe the depths, if you fail to get strikes at, or near, the surface. (A flycaster may have to use a sinking line to get down to the bottom of deep pools.)

And if you get a fish on, try to maneuver so that you are below him, leaving him no choice but to swim upstream. The additional burden thus placed upon the fish—that is, swimming against the current— will tire it more quickly. If you try to chase a fish downstream, especially if you are wading—you run a greater risk of slipping. Too, you have more time to work your way past obstructions as the slowed-down fish battles its way upstream.

Heavy rain—sometimes snow runoff, too—can be the despair of the stream and river fisherman. Reason: the water rises, washing mud and debris downstream. The water often becomes so roiled that you cannot see the fish, nor can they, in turn, see your bait or lure, regardless how well your offering may be presented.

Such annoying rain and bothersome soil runoff is usually worst in the spring. However, if you are lucky enough to be present and catch the early spring rain, following a dry season, then you may enjoy some fine sport with trout by fishing your bait or lure slow, and deep. But this good fishing will last only until the water becomes really roiled. After that, your only hope is to find another waterway, the upstream portion of which still has not been subjected to rain and runoff. Sometimes this will be a feeder stream, the current of which is slowed by beaver dams, or other natural obstructions.

Chapter 13
Lake Fishing

An experienced angler "reads" a lake with the same approach that he uses to evaluate a stream or river. For, once again, he is looking for the three conditions that determine good fishing water: namely, food, safety and comfort.

Much of this "reading" can be done at home. That is, a contour map will clearly reveal the presence of drop-offs and other fish-attracting sites. Such maps are frequently available, at little or no cost, from state fish commissions and other sources, and can quickly tell you what lakes in the area promise the best fishing. Ask at tackle stores, too, how to get such maps.

A contour map makes use of wavy lines to indicate bottom contours—and depths—as shown in *Figure 13–1*. Lines that are close together indicate deep water, and vice versa. Points A and B in the illustration, therefore, reveal quick drop-offs into deep water from a shoal area. In other words, these would be good places to expect natural food—hence game fish—to be present, as was discussed in the last chapter.

Note the feeder stream that empties into the lake at C. The mouth of this waterway, too, could be expected to deliver washed-down food to the lake, and therefore attract fish. Too, should it be a spring-fed stream, the colder water would attract trout to the entrance.

The small "island" of lines at D indicates a marked upthrust of the bottom: a reef. Reefs, like submerged rocks, grassy shoreline points that continue outward until they disappear beneath the surface, and other "underwater structures" (as they are sometimes called) warrant your particular attention. Such sites appeal to fish because they offer food, safety and comfort.

If you have no map, the shoreline often can be used to indicate whether a lake is "dead." A shore that is flat and devoid of growths seldom indicates good fishing. On the other hand, a steep shore with trees and undergrowth usually tells of deep water close by—and the

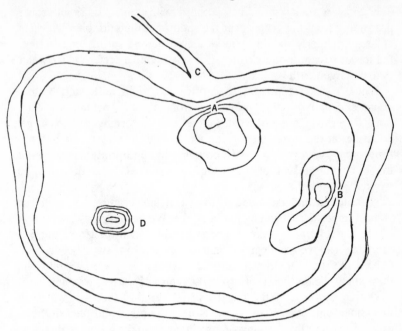

Figure 13–1 Contour Map

good possibility of moving water that can carry fallen insects and other food to waiting fish. Too, such an overgrown, steep bank provides cool shade, and likely an undercut bank (a result of the current), perhaps even holes, where fish can hide.

A shoreline point is always worthy of inspection since such an outstretched finger of land can interrupt water flow and cause a food-carrying and bait fish-disabling current at its extremity. Too, such points often continue into the lake as bars. And fish, particularly bass, like to work their way up onto such shoals to feed and bask—especially, should the bottom be grassy.

Largemouth bass, northern pike, muskellunge and walleyes also like to frequent shallow coves and bays that offer weed growths and lily pads in which to feed and hide. So look for these places, too, along a lake shore. Keep in mind that such fish feed upon minnows, insects, crayfish, frogs and other natural foods (see Chapter 3) and use such baits accordingly. Or strive to match such natural food, both in size and appearance, with artificial lures.

Is there a rocky shoreline, perhaps with some additional rocks protruding from the water, near the shore? Smallmouth bass like such areas, particularly should there be a cold bottom spring, or a spring-fed feeder stream in the vicinity. For smallmouths prefer colder water than do largemouth bass.

Where rocks are present food often lodges in holes and bottom crevices. Small fish find protection from currents behind boulders. And larger fish are attracted to the area accordingly. If you get no strikes at the surface, try going under—all the way to the bottom, if necessary, with your casts. To do this, add appropriate sinker weight to your natural bait offering. Or use artificial lures that can be worked beneath the surface.

A thorough understanding of the effect temperature has upon fish is most important when angling in a lake. We have already stated that a fish, like a human, becomes uncomfortable when the temperature is too high (above 70 degrees Fahrenheit) or too low (below 50). Should the water approach the freezing state, a fish may simply lie dormant at the bottom, waiting for the return of warmer weather.

During the heat of the day bass and certain other fish will seek deep holes and other cool places. Not so the pikes and panfish, however. Then, in the evening—sometimes at night—and again early the following morning, fish will return to the now cooled-off shallow areas to feed. This swimming pattern will vary with the seasons. Fish that are usually found in shallow water in spring and fall may swim in deeper water in summer and winter. (In summer, the deeper water keeps them cool; in winter it keeps them warm.)

The trick, then, is to discover at what comfort depth of the lake (or "thermocline," as it is called) the fish are on the day you have chosen to go fishing. This can be done in several ways. You can lower a fishing thermometer (or even an ordinary household type) into the lake to determine that depth which represents the optimum comfort zone. This will usually be within the range 50 to 65 degrees, although it may vary with certain species. Fishing thermometers are sold with detailed instructions how to use them.

A sometimes quicker, and easier, way to find the fish is by trolling. You can also cover a larger area this way, too. Use two lines, as shown in *Figure 13–2*. Troll one line shallow, the other deep. Begin the deep trolling by bumping the bait or artificial lure right along the bottom. Then, if no strikes are forthcoming, probe the waters above with increasingly shorter lines. In warm weather you may find

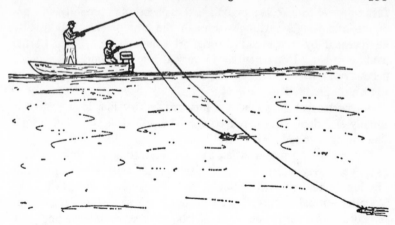

Figure 13–2

it necessary to go down forty feet, or more, to find the depth most comfortable for certain fish: walleyes, lake trout and landlocked salmon, for example.

This optimum fish depth, or thermocline, will vary not only with temperature, but also with the water's oxygen content. Too, in addition to providing them maximum comfort, fish are attracted to the thermocline because this layer is most productive of plankton, and hence the bait fish that feed upon such microscopic food.

Once you have found the thermocline it becomes simply a matter of continuing to fish that depth—and that portion—of the lake.

A regulation bait casting rod, equipped with a revolving type reel with level winding mechanism and a spool filled with 8 to 15 pound test line, is probably the tackle most widely used for fresh water trolling. Spoons and spinners are favorite trolling lures, although worms and other plastic artificials, deep-running plugs and weighted jigs—the latter sometimes tipped with a strip of natural bait, or pork rind—are used frequently, too.

Should your line develop twists from such trolling try using a keel type sinker before the bait or lure, or perhaps an additional series (barrel) swivel. You can sometimes straighten a badly twisted line by letting it all out, after removing the terminal rig, to untwist in a strong, going-away current, or in the wake of a fast-moving boat.

A good trolling speed often is found to be about equal to a man's fast walk. A trolled lure or bait that is "working" properly will undulate and wiggle invitingly through the water. This will usually be revealed by a continuing series of small, even twitches of the trolling rod tip. Don't hesitate to vary the speed, should this prove necessary to produce strikes. Then stick with that speed which seems to be most productive.

For surface trolling, about a hundred feet of line in the wake is usually sufficient. The depth of the lake will determine how much line will be required for deep trolling.

If you must go fishing when the temperature is very low, or very high, you likely will fare best by fishing with bait—deep. Since fish are sluggish under these conditions, do not make the retrieve fast.

Under normal temperature conditions you can cast and retrieve in the normal manner from a boat, or from shore, or while wading. It is advantageous to cast in fan-shaped zones, as shown in *Figure 13–3*. Begin by fishing out the zone closest to the casting position. Then move outward to the second zone, finally to the third and last.. This

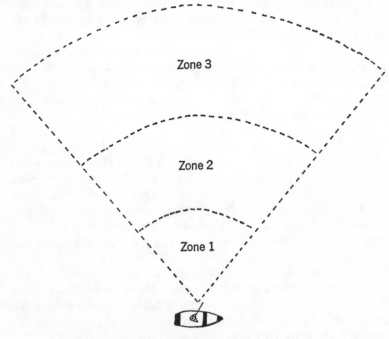

Figure 13–3   Zone Casting

method lessens the danger of scaring away fish in your immediate casting area. For some reason beginners often make the mistake of believing that the farther they cast out at the outset, the better will be their chances for getting a strike. To the contrary, a fish will tend to feel trapped—and dart away to the safety of deeper water, as a result—should one's cast set up a disturbance *beyond* the fish, so that the fish is between the disturbance and the shore.

The best retrieve to use while fishing a lake will vary somewhat with the kind of fish involved. Muskellunge and pike are swift and vicious predators. Hence for these fish, used to pouncing upon fleeing smaller fish, you should use a quick, erratic retrieve. Bass, on the other hand, seem to respond best to a slow-moving lure—and you will often be wasting your time if you don't cast it within close range of these fish. Picture a frog—a favorite bass food—leaping from a lily pad. The little amphibian will likely strike the surface with a gentle splash—then swim away by alternately kicking its legs, gliding forward from this momentum. So your surface lure should land, likewise, with a simulating light splash. The lure should be allowed to rest for several seconds (just as a frog often will rest, with only eyes and top of head protruding, before swimming off). You should then begin a retrieve that makes your bait or lure simulate the movement of a swimming frog. This can be done by alternately twitching the rod tip, then reeling in a few turns to take up slack, while the lure rests.

Do this, and you may quickly find yourself "in business" with Old Mr. Bass.

In summary, it will be the condition of a lake's bottom that will mainly determine the lake's value as a fishing site. Should there be present rocks, weedy bars and other obstructions beneath the surface, the chances are good that bait fish—and hence interested game fish— will congregate at these "fish hotels," where acquatic growths produce minute foods, and which provide shelter, for the smaller fish. A bare lake bottom generally means poor fishing.

If you cannot see the bottom from the surface, try using a glass-bottom bucket, or a skin diver's face mask. Should that fail, a rocky bottom can sometimes be located by lowering a sounding line attached to a heavy sinker. The weight will make a distinct *chink* when it encounters rock. And you can always refer to a contour map, of course, to find the type of bottom material, the drop-offs, channels, reefs and other submerged conditions that attract game fish.

Chapter 14
Salt Bay, Inlet
and River Fishing

Just as do their fresh water counterparts, many ocean fish seek the safety of shallow water to spawn. To do this the deep water fish come inshore. At certain seasons they pass through sea-connecting inlets, to enter salt bays and other estuarine (ocean tidal) areas. There are those sea fish, also, that frequent such coastal shallows—moving in and out with the tide to do this—to feed upon the teeming small saltwater bait fish and crustaceans (crabs, shrimps, etc.) that live in the estuary. Hence these salt bays and inlets and rivers can offer good fishing for the angler who either does not own a sea-worthy boat, or who cannot afford to rent or charter one.

Saltwater fishing is done, generally, in the same manner as the fresh water kind. That is, the angler presents in acceptable manner a natural bait or lure to fish that are present because of food, safety and comfort. Or, at least, some appealing combinations of these ideal fishing conditions. To do this the angler ordinarily uses tackle that not only is somewhat heavier, but which employs rustproof hardware. (The heavier tackle is used because saltwater fish are generally larger and stronger than the fresh water species.)

And in the salt a couple new factors make their appearance to influence the ideal fishing equation. These factors are wind and tide.

It is true that wind does play an important role inland, also: a strong wind can build up dangerous waves on a large lake, for example. But inland waters are usually protected by trees and hills—unlike the flat and open coastal reaches that often lie fully exposed for miles. Wind will not only make a coastal inlet, sound or river unsafe for small boat use, it can kick up such a fuss that fish which have come inshore to feed will hastily return to the depths—lest they become stranded, perhaps, in a bay from which the wind has blown most of the water, for example. Too, wind will roil the water so badly—stirring up bottom sediment in shallow estuarine areas—that it becomes difficult, if not impossible, for those fish that may remain to see a bait or lure when it is offered them. Nor, equally bad, can the angler see them, to direct his casts.

And in a strong wind a flycaster may as well stay home.

Tide can, and will, have an even greater effect than wind upon estuarine saltwater fishing. The effect, fortunately, is usually good.

The gravitational influence of the moon (mainly) and the sun causes the world's salt waters to rise and fall twice each day. Usually, this change amounts to perhaps only a difference of two or three feet in water level—although in some areas, like the Bay of Fundy of eastern Canada, the change may be twenty times that amount. Tide is vitally important to the saltwater angler because it creates current (water movement) that determines whether fish food will be available. And it changes water depths, hence access to such natural food by game fish.

When fishing coastal bays, gulfs and rivers it is good to keep in mind this rule of thumb: an incoming, or rising, tide generally results in oncoming (feeding) fish; an outgoing, or dropping, tide causes the natural food—and hence the pursuing game fish—to disappear. Reason for this: fish seem to have a built-in fear of being trapped, even stranded, by a dropping tide. A fish trapped in a shallow tide pool is at the mercy of the first passing bird or animal, including the human variety. And, of course, a stranded fish soon dies for lack of oxygen, which it can only get from water.

Many, indeed, have been the times that I have watched big tarpon swim in from the sea in Florida, on an incoming tide, to fan out over shallow bays and enter coastal rivers. You could hear these big silver horses sometimes a quarter mile away as they tore up the surface, feeding upon schools of fingerling mullet, and other natural food. Soon as the tide began a strong reversal, however, the tarpon invariably deserted the shoal areas. Often they spilled into small finger channels to do this, waterways that led back through the flats to the sea, and this made them ideal targets to cast to as they passed one's boat anchored upon the nearby shoal.

The angler who understands the habits of fresh water fish will quickly find himself at home in the salt. Drop-offs and holes still play the same role of bait basket, to attract the larger fish. Rocks and other bottom obstructions provide shelter from strong currents, as well as encouragement for the aquatic growths that feed and shelter small fish that attract game fish . . . and so on.

Just as the fresh water fisherman can usually purchase a contour map to indicate the presence of lake drop-offs, submerged islands, etc., so can the saltwater man resort to navigational charts for coastal waters. The saltwater map is easier to use, some anglers feel, because it mainly uses numerals to indicate water depth, in feet. The charts cost about $1.50 each, and cover a considerable area. If you cannot get the one you need from a tackle, or similar, shop, write to the U. S. Coast and Geodetic Survey, Rockville, Maryland 20850.

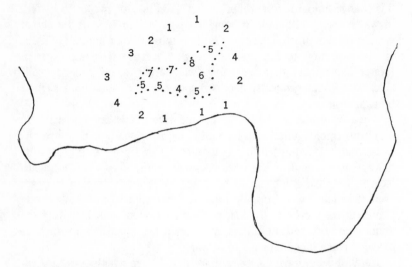

Figure 14–1   Typical Section of a U. S. Coast & Geodetic Survey Map

Figure 14–1 shows a typical section from a USC&GS map. Note how the constantly changing water-depth figures suddenly increase in value to indicate deeper water—in this case a small channel running through a bank, or shoal. Tide will sweep bait into such an abrupt drop-off, and game fish know this, and frequent such sites accordingly.

Consider *Figure 14–2*, which portrays a typical estuarine area. Before you read the explanations that follow, see if you can tell by yourself why each of the sites designated on this map should offer good fishing.

Site No. 1, the inlet to this salt bay, obviously is of special interest since every fish that enters the estuary from the sea to feed or spawn must move through this natural passage at least once. (Usually, it is twice, once to enter with a rising tide, then to depart as the tide flows outward again—although some fish will remain inside.) Sometimes an inlet is so narrow that an angler can cast nearly from one shore to

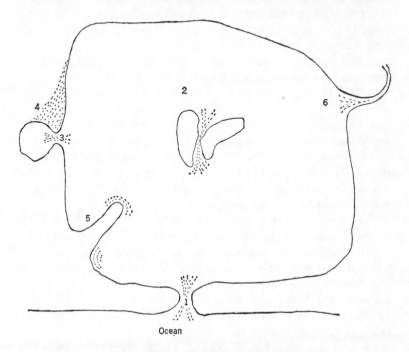

Ocean

Figure 14–2 Typical Estuarine Area

the other. This, of course, increases his chance for success even more.

Look at No. 2. Here the incoming and outgoing tide (current) is squeezed between two islands, to form a "race." Not only will this current tend to concentrate natural food at this site, to be carried toward waiting game fish, it also will likely prove so strong that it will hinder minnows, crabs, other natural foods that try to swim in it— thereby making it easier for hungry game fish to feed upon such offerings.

Would you be tempted to fish at No. 3, the narrow entrance to the cove? You should. For frequently fish will move into such places in search of food as the tide starts to rise. Another good time for you to be present would be during the last of the dropping (outgoing) tide. For then, as we have stated earlier, the fish will be moving outward again, to avoid being trapped inside the cove by insufficient water.

How about the marsh at No. 4? As the rising tide moves above the level of the shore, to flood the marsh grass, hungry minnows, crabs, etc., will swim upward and over the bank into the grass to forage for food. The larger game fish cannot follow into such shallows. So they wait wisely, instead, for the tide to drop again, to force this food back into the deeper water. Then the game fish swim hard against the shore, to feed upon the returning bait fish, etc., that come spilling back over the top of the bank. And that is where you should place your casts, too.

A Geodetic Survey chart for this area that we are considering would likely indicate a number of holes, cuts and channels where bait fish—and hence game fish—will concentrate at low tide. In the shallow Florida Bay area of the Keys, for example, snook and other fish will lie in such holes, waiting for the moving tide to carry shrimps and other natural foods to them.

Note the point of land that is indicated at position No. 5. As strong current strikes this obstruction an eddy is often set up that scoops out a bait-disabling—and holding—hole at the neck of the peninsula, where it joins with the mainland. There likely will be a second deep spot scoured out by the current as it sweeps past the opposite end of the point, too. Some game fish will work the eddy; others will prefer to lie close on the lee side of the point, in position to snatch any food that is carried past them by the current.

Look at the river, No. 6. The mouth of any river, canal, tidal creek, etc., can be a good bet on an outgoing tide. For then the current will wash bait fish, worms, crabs and other food to larger fish that have learned it pays to wait in position at the mouths of such connecting waterways.

Your USC&GS map will reveal not only water depths, but also the nature of the bottom. Are there any grassy areas indicated? Weakfish love such places. So do eels, croakers and certain other species. (Refer to Chapter 5.) Are there any rocky areas? Rockfish (striped bass), sheepshead and tautog prefer these. How about oyster and other shellfish beds? These attract channel bass (redfish), sea bass and porgies. Kingfish, flounders (especially) and spot like sand bottoms.

Should the estuary be a large one, you may have to explore it by trolling—just as was explained in the preceding chapter for fresh water lake fishing—to find whether fish are present, and, if so, at what depth. Just as before, you can troll two lines, varying the depth of these, to accomplish this exploration. Soon as you get a strike, of course, drop anchor and start to fish by casting to the same depth. Some anglers prefer to cast from a drifting boat to explore thus for fish. When making casts while drifting you will have to use lures of various weights (and perhaps different actions) to investigate the various depths. Best lure action usually results when you cast up-current—in the direction opposite to that in which the boat is drifting—or crosscurrent.

While trolling or drifting thus, look for patches of surface shadow, perhaps small areas of disturbed water, that may indicate schools of bait fish at, or slightly under, the surface. Sometimes the presence of seabirds can tip you to the presence of such game fish-attracting bait. Very often such schools of bait fish are concentrated, nervous. So don't cast into the midst of these little mullet, killifish, herring, spearing or whatever, else you may send them quickly bottomward.

Should the various fishing methods we have discussed so far prove unproductive, you can try "chum." The origin of this expression remains unknown. It means to attract fish by grinding up edible substances—usually other fish, particularly those of the oily variety, like menhaden—then casting such remnants upon the water. In ordinary use, the word chum means a close friend. And perhaps this is what the gullible fish mistake to be an angler's motivation, as they follow the chum slick and come within casting range of his baited hook, or artificial lure.

One of the easiest ways to chum is to purchase a frozen package of trash fish, or other offal (fish entrails, etc.) from a fish-packing house. A five-pound chunk of such chum, when placed inside a sack and lowered to the bottom with a stout cord, can require an hour or more to melt slowly. Meanwhile, it produces an oily line that is carried away by wind or current—sometimes for a mile or more— and striped bass, sharks and a host of other saltwater fish will be attracted. (If you get no strikes within twenty minutes, or so, haul up the chum and move to another location.)

Some anglers prefer to create a mixture of crabs, mussels or most anything else (even tinned sardines, dog and cat food, bread or oatmeal) when fish are not available for chum use. This "soup" is then poured overboard.

Probably the sportiest way to chum is to throw out small live fish, then use one of these—or a matching lure—to catch the game fish, when these appear. I have seen live pilchards used in this manner, in Florida, to lure record-size amberjack to the surface. These were then caught with streamer flies.

Fishing craft, notably shrimp boats, have a habit of dumping overboard a wide variety of unwanted fish that are invariably caught in the trawl net. This is usually done offshore, to avoid littering shorelines with dead fish. And if you fish in the vicinity of such king-size "chum pots" you may have good success, indeed.

To a lesser extent, commercial shellfishermen serve the same purpose when they disturb the bottom as they dig for clams and oysters. Little crabs and other food tidbits are disturbed and in turn attract hungry game fish. You can sometimes achieve this same effect by using your underway boat slowly to pull a lowered anchor across the bottom, should you have no chum available. Keep in mind, however, that when you do this you are apt to destroy important fish habitat.

Some anglers have no access to boats for fishing salt bays, inlets and rivers. They must content themselves by fishing from shore, from bridges, docks and seawalls, etc. This angling can prove quite competitive. The best places are invariably claimed, often by elderly anglers with nothing else to do—even if this should call for getting up before daybreak to insure a fishing space.

About all one can do under circumstances like this is to go fishing during those hours—mealtime, nighttime, etc.—and conditions (bad weather, etc.) that are least attractive to other anglers. You may be surprised how comfortable—and productive—it can be to fish at night. For then fish seem to be less cautious. Bait fish venture into the shallows, where they are followed boldly by striped bass and other game fish.

Meanwhile, try to learn why the most successful bridge and shore fishermen enjoy this distinction. If they won't talk (some can be grudgingly secretive), watch when, and how, they fish. There is much more to such fishing than merely lowering a baited hook.

Chapter 15
Surf, Pier and Jetty Fishing

Comparatively few surf fishermen are fortunate enough to own a "beach buggy"—a four-wheel-drive vehicle capable of carrying them and their tackle over sand without becoming stuck. Hence most surfers—like those anglers who fish inland streams—are obliged to park their cars, as close to the water as possible, then carry with them everything they will need to go fishing.

Such equipment will include the inevitable long surf rod—or, sometimes, a husky spinning stick, instead. Both shafts will be of tubular fiber glass, although some bamboo surf rods are also used. Each will measure from about nine to twelve feet, depending upon the height, strength and casting ability of the user. These sticks should be equipped with stainless steel guides and reel seats.

The reel for the surf rod will likely be of the wide spool type, capable of holding at least 150 yards of 30 pound breaking test line. (Lines of 20, even 15 pound, strength are easier to use and nearly as effective in the hands of a good fisherman.) Some surf reels hold twice this amount.

The brake, or drag, will usually be of the "star" type, easily adjusted by one finger of the reel hand, even while pumping in a fish. And the reel probably will have no level-wind provision, although some surfers prefer to use the lighter bait casting reels that do employ this feature.

The spinning reel, if one is used, should likewise be of large size, corrosion proof and capable of storing about 250 yards of 20 pound line (400 yards of 15 pound). It should have a smooth, dependable drag. (Some spinning reel drags fail to meet this requirement.)

The line on the surf reel can be either braided or solid (monofilament) nylon, or it can be of Dacron. Mono is used nearly always on spinning reels.

Leaders should be of stainless steel, preferably the braided kind. Or, heavy—30 to 100 pound test—monofilament can be used, instead. Leaders are generally from twelve to eighteen inches in length (to facilitate casting) and are often used in connection with a three-way swivel. A "fish finder" terminal connection is also popular.

Hooks used by surfers vary in size from perhaps 1/0 to 5/0. These, too, should preferably be of stainless steel.

For bait, small fish like fingerling mullet, menhaden, herring, etc., work well, live or dead. Other good natural baits are eels, worms, crabs, shrimps, clams and squid. (Refer to Chapter 3.)

Metal squids and heavy spoons are favorite artificials, since these are easy to cast and closely imitate in size and action the flashing bait fish that beach-prowling gamesters feed upon. The comparatively new plastic lures—eels, in particular—do well in the surf.

A pair of chest-high waders must also be included in your equipment, should you fish when the weather is cold, even chill, as many dedicated surfers do. You may be able to get by with cheap plastic waders. But if the weather is really raw, nothing takes the place of impregnated rubber waders with insulated boot feet. Down-filled underwear—likely outerwear, too—may be necessary under such conditions, also. For the winds that often sweep ocean beaches from fall to spring can really bite deeply.

An impregnated rubber rain parka can perform welcome double duty under such penetrating chill wind conditions. But don't overdress to the point where casting freedom is sacrificed. In warm weather, of course, you need wear only a pair of old duck pants, with sneakers; perhaps only a bathing suit.

You will need a tackle box. And an old-fashioned market basket, with carrying handle, can prove handy for transporting lunch, thermos, bait, etc. A belt, or apron, type cup (seat) for your rod butt will make for easier holding of the long stick as you stand alertly at the water's edge, waiting for a strike. A sandspike (i.e., a hollow metal tube of sufficient diameter so the rod butt can be slid into it; you can make one of these yourself) will hold the otherwise cumbersome rod upright while you change bait, etc. A small folding camp chair can be a blessing. And a gaff, even a short-handled one, can prevent last-minute loss of a thirty- to fifty-pound channel bass, or some other large fish, in the surf.

A long-handled gaff will be required, very likely, if you fish from jetties. And don't hesitate to strap a pair of creepers (cleats) to your boots. For otherwise you may suffer a nasty spill on the slimy, slippery jetty rocks.

Such conveniences, of course, all represent additional weight that the surfman must carry to the fishing site—and then on to other locations, as he moves along the beach, seeking fish. How many of these conveniences he enjoys, therefore, will depend upon his willingness—and strength—to take them along.

To surf cast either a conventional or a spinning rod, grasp the stick with one hand (your right, if you are right-handed, as I shall presume; if not, vice versa) at a convenient position above the reel. The other hand holds the rod at, or near, the bottom of the butt section, to provide casting leverage when the rod tip is brought up, and over, later.

Walk to the water's edge. (With today's efficient casting tackle it should not be necessary for you to wade out into the waves.) Hold the rod horizontal—about two feet above your right shoulder—and approximately parallel to the earth. Turn your body so that an imaginary line—running from one shoulder to the other—points seaward, toward the spot where you want the cast to end.

Now, with the reel in free spool condition (thumb pressure is preventing the spool from turning, or, if you are spinning, the bail has been pushed open [back] and the rod hand forefinger is holding the line) and the lure hanging straight down, two to three feet beneath the rod tip, bring the rod smartly up and over. This is done with a snap, as the left hand pulls the rod butt down, and the right arm and shoulder simultaneously push the upper part of the long stick upward.

The rod tip should make a long—and powerful—yet smooth arc, from about three o'clock to ten o'clock, as you follow through with the cast, swiveling your hips to keep the plane (direction) of the arc aimed at the target. When the rod tip approaches the ten o'clock position (and this is approximate; your particular method of casting will be the determining factor here) the thumb pressure—or hooked forefinger line-holding position, if you are spin fishing—is released sufficiently to allow the now heavily flexed (i.e., power-loaded) rod to send the lure hurtling toward its objective, yet without allowing the revolving reel spool to overrun and backlash.

Where and when you go will usually determine your success as a surf fisherman. Admittedly, it can be a soul-refreshing experience—for the awed inland angler, particularly—to stand fishing alone at the edge of a sparkling ocean; to hear the boom of surf, the shrill cries of seabirds, the muted song of the wind as it blows through the grassy hair of tall dunes. But such sights and sounds do not produce the thrilling tug at the end of the angler's line, nor can he take these sensations home, to be eaten.

So it is often best to make inquiries beforehand where and when to go. Ask local tackle shop operators, the fishing editors of newspapers, anyone who may be in a position to help. Cars parked along roads adjacent to the sea are often an indication of the presence of surf fishermen. Talk to them.

Sometimes, as you drive along an ocean-paralleling highway, you can observe schools of bait fish close to shore. Should these small fish be leaping nervously upward now and then, there likely are blues, striped bass, mackerel, snook or other game fish attacking them from underneath. And, should there be gulls and other seabirds present, diving down to snatch up torn remnants floating on the surface, you can be certain there are larger fish feeding on this bait. The thing to do then is to park your car quickly and cast a bait, or lure, close as possible to this feeding activity.

If you must fish a strange area, without benefit of information beforehand, it is well to know how to "read" a beach. This is best done when the tide is low, the water is calm and clear, and you can stand atop a sand dune, cliff or some other elevation. (Even an ocean-fronting hotel room can be used, if necessary; and here a pair of binoculars will help.)

You should look for holes, sloughs (stretches of deep water between—and usually parallel to—the beach and a sand bar), rocks, wrecks, cuts or channels that allow tides to surge in and out through bars; any bottom contour, in fact, that may influence the movement and swimming ease of fish, and the availability of food and cover.

A break in a sand bar, for example, will allow water to rush through. This stronger than usual water movement will make swimming difficult for bait fish, thereby attracting from the nearby deeper water larger fish that prey upon such smaller ones. Too, the current will wash out crustaceans and shellfish that game fish feed upon.

Just as in fresh water, a drop-off will collect bait fish, crabs, sand fleas and other food. And a rock, reef or other bottom obstruction provides not only an opportunity for food, but also a welcome resting place for fish in its lee. Should the tide be up, and the surface rough, you may still often identify such deeper places by the darker blue, or green, color of the water. Too, if waves break (i.e., form white water) on an outer bar, then stop cresting and curling until they once more break upon the shore, this is an indication of intervening deep water: a slough, gulley or hole between the bar and the beach. If the breakers take place *only* against the shore it is a sign there is no bar— in which case you would not expect the existence of a fish-using cut, or swimway, of course. Again, if there is continuing white water in one place, this can reveal the presence of a rock, reef, even a wreck close beneath the surface.

Waves crashing upon, and over, an exposed rock can wash free crabs and other tidbits for waiting game fish—stripers, especially. Cast as close as possible to such an exposed rock, also on both sides. Should the rock be slightly submerged, make your retrieve begin somewhat beyond, so the bait or lure swims back invitingly, just above the rock.

Keeping in mind the importance of water movement, it follows that other potentially good fishing sites would be tidal bay, lagoon or canal entrances; points of land; rocky shores; breakwaters and jetties. A map will come in handy, therefore, in planning the trip. And, once you have "read" a particular beach, you should try to keep in mind the most promising places—the bar cuts, holes, etc.—to be probed later, when the tide is up again, or perhaps at night. (Fishing improves, as a rule, after dark.) Unfortunately, save for rocks and wrecks, the sloughs and other fish-influencing conditions that you may discover along an ocean beach can, and will, change markedly with weather conditions. What may be a good hole one day, within easy casting range from the beach, may be only an unbroken—hence fishless— sand bottom the next.

After more than a quarter century of casting baits and lures from ocean beaches I have discovered, as have most other surfmen, that the two best times of day to fish are early morning—for about two hours, starting just before dawn—and from about two hours before sundown, on into the night, depending upon tide conditions. There are some areas where the fish may strike throughout the day, especially in late fall and early spring, but this happy condition is not common, unfortunately.

Tides change twice daily and it is always good practice to fish when the extent of such change is maximum. Two good times, for example, are when a low tide is starting to rise again, or a high tide is starting to drop. A still, or "slack," tide is generally the worst—although there can be exceptions. There seems to be most fish movement, and interest in feeding, when the tide is moving (i.e., causing a current). As a rule, a high tide is most productive when fishing a beach where there are shallow areas: sand bars, rocky reefs, etc. Conversely, a low tide is generally best when casting to drop-offs and holes, other deep water pockets, around a rock jetty and along a beach that slopes sharply to deep water.

Another surfman's rule of thumb is: onshore wind means good fishing; offshore wind, potentially poor fishing. Reason: a high surf from an onshore wind brings bait fish, hence game fish, in close. It also attracts game fish by churning up the bottom, exposing crabs and other food. Some of the best surf fishing that I've enjoyed has taken place immediately before, and after, coastal storms (but not when the water is dirty). In fact, I've seen non-fishermen walk the Florida beaches, shortly after hurricanes, to pick up large game fish, many of them still alive. Apparently these fish were cast unexpectedly ashore after they had entered the surf, to take advantage of the food-producing rough water action.

Many beginning surf fishermen make the mistake of trying to cast out too far, when this is not needed. There are times, it is true, especially during an offshore wind, when the bait fish—and therefore the game fish—remain quite far out, and long casts may prove necessary. But keep in mind that surf fishing is just that: fishing in the surf, since the main idea is to capture fish that come into the surf to feed, for reasons that we have already discussed. Often have I seen thousands of little bait fish—another way of saying darting, gorging game fish (blues, in particular; these gluttons will fill their stomachs to bursting, then rid themselves of the contents by regurgitation, to begin over)—so close that the eager, feeding fish were nearly thrown bodily onto the beach by the breaking waves. (By the way, I've seen huge sharks feeding thus, also; so close that they pitched and rolled in the first breakers, those nearest the shore.)

Once you have cast out a bait, and the sinker has had time to settle firmly into the bottom, you should fish with a taut line—since this will telegraph the first nibble. (Not all surf fish strike hard.) The rod tip should be held at about 45 degrees above the horizon—but not too high to prevent you from making a sudden strike by bringing the rod back even farther. The line will be least subject to tugging wave action when the rod is held thus.

The waves will gradually wash your bait back toward the beach. Each time you feel the sinker thus dislodged you should take up the slack anew, in anticipation of a strike. When the sea has thus "fished out" the retrieve for you there is little else you can do save reel in the remaining line, inspect the bait to make sure it is still of ample size, and well hooked, then cast it out again.

If you are fishing with a spoon, feather, plug or other artificial surface or diving lure, remember that ocean fish are used to pursuing swift bait fish. So make your retrieve an active one accordingly. This can be done by reeling in swiftly, pausing at intervals, perhaps aiding this action by twitching the rod tip—maybe even sweeping the rod sharply upward and backward now and then.

A fast retrieve is ordinarily not used when fishing a plastic eel, a lure that is probably the most deadly of all the saltwater artificials. In this case the speed of the return should be that which allows the eel to undulate invitingly from side to side—and up and down—as if it were alive. If you make a few practice retrieves in clear water, at various speeds, you will be able to determine at what speed this fine lure works best. The easiest eels to use are those that have some action built in, or installed by the angler after purchase. (For an example of the latter case, refer to *Figure 3–11,* which shows how a block tin squid may be added to provide a weighted head, and hence improved swimming action, for an eel bait.)

Sometimes it may prove necessary to bump a plastic eel along the bottom—or even to slide it there for a short distance—to provoke an otherwise cautious fish into striking.

The bait fisherman should use a pyramid sinker when fishing over a sand bottom, since the sharp edges of this weight are intended to allow it to bury itself, and hence hold better. Obviously, a rounded sinker should be used on a rocky bottom, to prevent snagging and possible need for breaking one's line. Again, there will be times—when using a "fish finder" terminal rig, for example—when a sinker with a hole through its center (i.e., an egg sinker) will serve the angler best.

Once a fish is hooked in the surf you can usually enjoy yourself by letting him run, by listening to the happy groan of the reel. This is why surfmen use reels of large capacity: they are standing at the edge of a big ocean, and the determined fish is going to make instinctively for the depths to escape. Of course, should there be danger of getting your line snagged, even cut off, by rocks, kelp beds, etc., you cannot indulge yourself by letting the fish run thus to wear himself out. Then you must "put the stick" to him, instead: use as much drag as you safely dare; pump him ashore as soon as possible.

Sometimes you can lead a fish away from threatening obstructions by walking or running along the beach, in an opposite direction. There may be those times, too, when you will find it necessary to follow along a beach, after a shark or other big fish, to prevent the catch from taking all the line from your reel.

Chapter 10 describes how to beach a fish, both with and without the aid of net or gaff. If the waves are high, or there is a strong undertow (outgoing current), it will be prudent not to try and horse the fish shoreward against such increased pull. Reel and pump only when a wave carries the struggling fish toward you—not away. If necessary, move along the beach in an effort to guide the fish away from the undertow, before attempting to beach it. If you fail to take such precautions the added strain may cause your leader or line to break.

Jetties and breakwaters can provide good fishing when these are encountered along an ocean beach. For such obstructions interrupt the normal flow of water, thereby creating food-carrying and bait fish-disabling currents that work to the advantage of the knowledgeable angler, as already discussed. Jetties usually consist of piled-up rocks, placed to protect beaches from erosion. Breakwaters are built to protect inlets and harbor entrances; to prevent these waterways from becoming filled with current-borne sand and mud. Both obstructions may extend out from shore for a considerable distance, thereby enabling an angler to reach water ordinarily beyond casting range from shore.

Jetties can prove dangerous. It is easy to slip upon the slimy rocks. So wear boot, or shoe, creeper irons. Breakwaters usually have a flat top, hence can serve as ideal platforms for casters.

Maximum current movement takes place, as might be expected, at the deep outer end of such structures. Often a strong tide rip so set up will make swimming difficult for bait fish, and therefore will attract game fish, in the usual manner.

Certain rocky shore points can have the same effect. And a boulder-strewn cove—should there be one adjacent to such a point—is also well worth exploring with your casts.

A fishing pier is a structure that thrusts itself outward from the beach. It usually stands atop sturdy pilings, and has a deck from which anglers can fish. An admission fee is ordinarily charged. Bait, tackle and other fishermen's needs can often be purchased, and generally water is provided for cleaning your fish.

The main difficulty with fishing piers is that they quickly become overcrowded when the fish are biting well. On the other hand, it can provide a pleasant way to spend a lazy day, talking with congenial fellow anglers, and generally enjoying yourself—even if the fish do not bite regularly.

Chapter 16
Ocean Fishing

The ocean is big—and potentially dangerous. Caution should be your constant consideration, therefore, when fishing offshore in your own, or a rented, small boat . . . a practice that has become popular. Your craft should be equipped with at least one anchor and suitable line. And there should be other Coast Guard-recommended safety equipment aboard, including an ample supply of spare fuel. Nor should you disregard the value of extra water and food, for emergency use. And don't fish alone.

It is best to have two motors, so there will be at least one of these functioning to bring you safely back to port, when necessary. A two-way radio, even a small set, can be a lifesaver, too. And you should tell at least one responsible person ashore where you intend to fish, and when you expect to return. (Then be sure to advise that person when you *do* return.)

It is wise, also, to have an understanding how weather, and other changing conditions, can affect an ocean angler's safety. You may, for instance, guide your skiff seaward through some inlet with no difficulty, on an outgoing tide. The sun likely is shining, warm and friendly. The sea is down, blue-green and sparkling, perhaps calm as a lake. The salt air is clean and invigorating. A beautiful day for fishing, indeed, with an offshore wind for a bonus—to provide an ideal lee for trolling parallel to the beach.

Time passes quickly in such a serene, happy setting. But it takes only a few hours for the tide to change. When you decide to return you may discover—to your horror—that a severe chop, waves impossible for your small boat to cope with, has developed at the mouth of the inlet. Reason: the wind is still off the land, but now the tide has changed and is flowing shoreward, against the wind. Should you try to re-enter the inlet under these conditions one of the towering, following seas would quickly prove too much for your small boat: water would come spilling in over the low transom.

What to do? Risk being sent thus to the bottom? At best, your craft will likely be hurled against the jetty rocks, out of control, with subsequent loss of it, your tackle, other contents. Even worse, you and anyone with you, could be drowned—even should you attempt to land on the beach.

You are in trouble, captain! You should have considered such a possibility before you left port . . .

In this case you would have done better by chartering a boat, replete with captain and mate. Such charters cost from about $75 to $125 per full day, depending upon geographical location, although half-day trips are usually available, too, and often you can share cockpit space, and hence the charter fee, with up to five other anglers. Even cheaper, are the so-called "headboats," large craft that take upward of fifty anglers at a time offshore to troll and drift-fish. They charge as little as four or five dollars per half day, and provide the tackle and bait for this.

The ocean fisherman can get by, quite often, with fresh water spinning, fly and bait casting and trolling tackle. It is best, however, to use somewhat heavier equipment in each case. For in the sea one never knows what kind—or *size*—of fish may strike next. I know of a Florida light tackle angler who landed a forty-pound sailfish with a spinning rod and 6 pound test line. But this man would be the first to tell you that he was merely lucky to get away with this.

Surface trolling is the most popular form of offshore angling. And for good reason. You can tow a ballyhoo or other natural bait in your wake (Chapter 3 explains how to rig such a bait)—or perhaps a big spoon, plug, feather or plastic lure—and take marlin, sailfish, kingfish, mackerel, bonito, tuna—to name but a few of the species that habitually come to, or near, the surface of coastal waters to feed and spawn.

The ocean fisherman can also enjoy fine sport by underwater trolling, by bottom (i.e., still) fishing, by drifting and by "deep jigging." (Each of these methods will be explained.)

A medium-action hollow glass spinning rod between 7 and 8½ feet long, with matching open- or closed-faced spinning reel loaded with several hundred yards of 8 to 12 pound monofilament line, will cast lures up to about an ounce. This outfit will permit you to handle average ocean fish like blues, mackerel, small dolphin, etc. A 9- to 11-foot, two-handed type tubular glass spin rod with more backbone (stiffer action) and an open-faced reel full of 20 pound test line may prove necessary to handle sailfish and other heavier sea fish, however.

A fly rod from 8 to 9½ feet, one with suitable backbone (stiffness), and a large-capacity single-action reel having at least 150 yards of backing line, in addition to the usual fly line, will serve for most off-shore fishing. Some flymen prefer rods as short as seven feet, quite stiff, better to pump back to the surface tuna and other deep water fish that have a tendency to go deep—and remain deep (sometimes dying in the depths) when hooked. If you are going after billfish and similar large species, a big fly reel with a dependable built-in brake (drag) becomes a must. Most of my angling acquaintances fish off-shore with two fly rods rigged and ready for use: one equipped with a floating line, for surface fishing, the other with a sinking line, for fishing as much as thirty feet below the surface. (Some specialists fish eighty feet or more down, to reach bottom fish on reefs, and use special lead-core and other weighted lines, in connection with their sinking fly lines, to do this. This new style of ocean fly fishing sport was inaugurated in California waters, and is still limited to the West Coast, mainly.)

The angler who prefers to cast bait and artificials offshore can get by nicely with a medium-action bait rod about 5 or 6 feet long. The level-wind reel that is usually used with such a stick should have a capacity of at least 150 yards of 12 to 15 pound test line. For heavier fishing, 20 to 30 pound line, with matching bait casting rod and reel, can be used. Heavier mono tends to give more trouble (from kinks, and general difficulty of keeping it evenly on the reel) than does the lighter variety.

Leaders for spinning and bait casting will vary from 6 to 18 inches in length. They are sometimes of stainless steel, either solid or braided wire, to serve as a safeguard against sharp-toothed ocean fish. Leaders of heavy monofilament often serve as well, or better, especially when used as shock leaders when casting flies.

Surface lures that are popular include darters and various other styles of plugs like big poppers (popping bugs in the case of fly casting). Feather and nylon jigs, spoons, metal squids, spinners and swimming plugs are used underwater.

Artificials may not perform as well as natural bait for bottom-feeding fish like grouper, cabezon, tomcod, tautog, porgies, sea bass, etc. For these, live or cut bait can be used, as described in Chapter 3.

For average trolling a 6- to 7-foot stiff (heavy-action) hollow glass rod with detachable rubber-covered hardwood butt is generally used.

The reel has no level-wind feature and it holds 200 or 300 yards of 30 pound test line. Heavier, so-called "big game" trolling outfits, employ a rod with roller tip, the butt having a cross-slotted nock that engages the matching gimbal of a fighting chair. The angler is usually strapped fast to this chair, and works reels in sizes from about 9/0 up to 16/0. Lines are as strong as 39-thread (i.e., the 130 pound breaking class).

A typical trolling leader would be 9 feet of No. 6 or 7 stainless wire, with a hook 6/0 to 9/0 in size. It is advisable to use dull-finish leader wire and swivels. If not, mackerel, kings and other swift ocean fish may strike at the flash of such metal, instead of the bait or lure, and cut the line. Refer to *Figure 2–6*, how to leader-tie a saltwater lure to insure best swimming action.

Most small boaters troll two "flat lines" for offshore fishing. (You can troll four lines simultaneously, should you have outriggers mounted on a small boat. These are hinged poles, usually of light aluminum, that can be swung outward, one on each side, at about a 45-degree angle above the horizon. Outriggers are by no means a must, however.) One flat line should be let out until the bait or lure is about three boat lengths astern; the other is then positioned perhaps an additional couple lengths behind that. Trolling speed will vary with water conditions, but should be such that the natural or artificial bait swims and skips invitingly at the surface, perhaps now and then plunging through a wave in the boat's wake.

You can help lure action while trolling—that is, help the spoon, feather, etc., dive and wiggle more realistically—by periodically bringing the rod tip up and back, about a yard each time, after which the tip is lowered once more toward the wake, ready for striking. Fish a big surface popper in this manner—a large floating plug with hollowed-out face—and you can set up a tantalizing fuss at the surface that will drive dolphin, barracuda, jacks, kingfish and other ocean residents wild. It is not unusual, either, for such bottom species as snapper and grouper to lose all control at such a sight—and zoom up from fifty feet or more below, to explode high into the air, with lure in mouth, like a leaping sailfish or tarpon!

The reel drag should be set very lightly while trolling—especially, if the two rods being fished are unattended (i.e., resting in gunwale holders). For a wahoo or other darting ocean fish can strike so swiftly that a too tightly braked line will part with a snap.

Most ocean fish manage to hook themselves when they strike a trolled bait. All you need do is raise the rod tip once or twice to make sure the barb is firmly seated. In some cases, however, notably billfish, you should "drop back" before making the strike. A sailfish or marlin, for example, will likely surface close behind, or perhaps alongside, a skipping ballyhoo bait. The eager fish will then tap the bait with its long bill, apparently to kill it. If you free-spool the reel when you observe this taking place, thereby causing the bait suddenly to halt its forward movement and sink helplessly, the billfish likely will be fooled into believing it has killed its prey, and thus proceed to gobble it up.

Below the surface trolling is done for king mackerel (kingfish) and other ocean species that swim in the depths as well as at the surface. Weighted natural bait, cut in strips or used whole (see *Figure 3–14*), feather and nylon jigs; a dead eel, or a plastic replica; wobbling spoons and other artificial lures, can be used. These are often rigged behind a keel type sinker of the type shown in *Figure 3–13*.

The bottom, or still, fisherman anchors his boat and lowers—usually all the way to the bottom of the sea—a bait which he has reason to believe will prove acceptable to the fish in a particular area. Should a strike not result he may resort to chumming. (See Chapter 14.) *Figure 16–1* shows several terminal rigs that are popular for bottom fishing.

The drift fisherman lowers a bait in a similar manner—but he depends upon the drifting boat to carry his bait through the water, over a considerable area. The bait is positioned somewhere between the near-surface and the bottom while doing this. (Usually the bait is weighted well and positioned to move along just above the bottom.)

This bait may be a whole ballyhoo, mullet or other fish—or a fillet (strip) cut from such fish. Small yellowtail, blue runners, pinfish and similar live bait fish can prove very effective when these are allowed to swim slowly, and naturally, in the depths beneath the drifting boat. Sailfish are taken repeatedly this way in Florida waters.

"Deep jigging" is a relatively new kind of ocean fishing sport, one that may have originated in Florida. A feather or nylon jig, usually two or three ounces in size, is allowed to sink straight down—as much as 200 feet, if necessary—to the bottom. The lure is then pumped and reeled quickly back to the surface. This is accomplished with a continuing series of vigorous upward sweeps of the sturdy rod, slack line, meanwhile, being reeled in quickly after each such upswing.

Deep jigging is done with both medium and heavy tackle. If

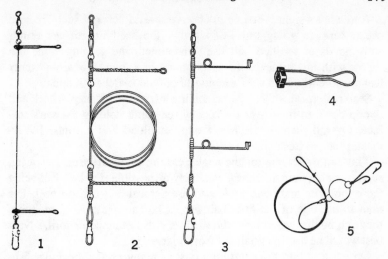

Figure 16–1 (1) J.T. saltwater spinning top and bottom rig, (2) Light-weight spinning rig, (3) Ready rig, (4) Quick rig, (5) Fireball rig (Courtesy of Virginia Dept. of Conservation & Economic Development)

medium weight spinning or bait casting rods are used, these should have ample backbone to withstand the strain of such violent jigging.

The ultimate of ocean fishing—where this writer is concerned—is to come upon a large school of surfaced fish—wildly feeding bluefish, tuna, mackerel and other species—then cast artificial lures to these from a boat drifting nearby.

To find such surfaced fish, watch for feeding birds. Binoculars will help you do this. When you spot such bird activity, hasten to the site. But *do not* run close with your boat. For if you do, the vibrations of the propeller can frighten the fish, send them plunging bottomward, beyond reach. Instead, establish in which direction the school may be moving, then wait—with motor off—for the fish to approach within casting range. Should the school not be moving, you have no choice but to approach with idling motor, hoping for the best. Shut off the engine as soon as you are within range. Sometimes the craft's momentum, or a stern wind, will help make such a cautious approach.

Don't wait squarely in the path of an approaching school. For the fish will then see you, and may become frightened. Instead, try to position yourself on the upwind side—if there is a wind—so the school will pass within easy casting range.

And what a sight it can be to observe several acres of such frenzied ocean carnage going on! Periodically, the seething surface erupts with clouds of terrified bait fish. Undaunted, the gorging game fish follow with mighty leaps that carry them in a long, low arc—twenty feet or more—to land with a mouthful of food snatched in midair.

Seabirds, meanwhile, are screaming excitedly as they wheel and swoop down to fight over the bloody remnants staining the sea's surface. Overall there is the heavy odor of blood and entrails. It permeates the sea-fresh air.

This can be Utopia for the angler casting artificial lures. Use a jig, spoon or plug that simulates, as closely as possible, the bait fish being fed upon. The man who prefers to use natural bait can do no better than to use one of the little bait fish, if he can get one. (Sometimes they can be dip-netted from the surface, either stunned or torn.) Next best would be a strip of bait cut from a larger fish.

Do not cast into the churning mass, as many excited beginner fishermen do. To do so can get your line cut in an instant. And you may even frighten the fish, put down the whole school! Even if you are using the customary foot or so of solid or braided stainless steel wire, or a similar length of 30 to 100 pound test monofilament shock leader, the chances are still excellent that your line will be quickly cut by the bodies of the darting game fish, particularly should the fish be mackerel, kings, tuna or bonito. For these species all have bony body ridges, near the tail, that can part a line like a knife.

Instead, cast to the near edge of the school—as close to the activity as you can. Time your retrieve so the bait or lure moves back toward the boat the moment it strikes the water. Try to keep in mind that the main consideration here is lifelike movement: both the pursued and the pursuers move swiftly in the ocean. So fish the retrieve to make your offering dart and dive through the water, like a bait fish trying desperately to escape its pursuer.

The strike will come in no uncertain manner: a vicious sock. Set the hook firmly with two or three quick, short backward jerks of the rod tip. Don't overdo it, and risk pulling the barb from the speeding fish's mouth.

Then let him run—or, more likely, dive deep.

Meanwhile, *decrease* drag with an increase of line being run off the reel by the departing fish, as has already been explained. When the fish tires and turns, and you have him coming back toward the boat, then you can once more safely increase the reel braking.

Appendix

How to Make Your Own Wading Shoes

Those anglers who cannot afford felt sole shoes and boots, as a safe-guard against slipping while wading, can use ordinary carpet material, instead. It will serve nearly as well. In fact, there are those fishermen who feel that carpet soles do an even safer job than felt soles.

You will need these materials: about two square feet of carpet; some shoemaker's rubber cement; a pair of scissors; a putty knife (or small piece of wood, etc.) to spread the cement; the pair of shoes, or waders, to be soled.

Scrap carpeting can be purchased cheaply from stores. Often the manager will give you enough such remnant material to make several pairs of soles; these to serve as spares. Too, you can sometimes salvage such carpet material, at no cost, from refuse piles where new homes and apartments have recently been carpeted.

Do not use carpet material that is bonded to a foam rubber backing. And avoid using short-piled and waterproof "outdoor" type carpet material. The old-fashioned kind, with the pile woven right into the carpet backing, is best. However, modern carpet material that is thermally or chemically bonded to a backing of jute will serve nicely, too.

For a dollar, or less, you should be able to purchase from a shoe repair shop sufficient rubber cement to fasten securely a dozen carpet soles.

Place each wading shoe, or wader boot, in turn upon the carpet (with its backing side up) and mark upon the carpet the outline of the sole. Cut out the soles, using a sharp pair of scissors. It is a good idea to outline and cut out several pairs at this time, for additional use later. Note that if it is a pair of wader boots that you are intending to sole, you must separate (cut off) the heel from the sole before it can be cemented. For on boots the heel piece must be fitted separately.

Next, use the putty knife to spread an ample quantity of cement, covering both the bottom surface(s) of the shoe or boot and the backing side of the carpet soles. The carpet may absorb much of the cement, but this needn't disturb you.

After waiting about ten minutes (follow directions of the cement manufacturer, or ask the shoemaker how long to wait) fit the two glued surfaces carefully together. Press the carpet sole firmly down against the bottom of wader shoe or boot, applying finger pressure from the center outward, toward the edges of the sole. This will help force out any air pockets that may have developed.

Your wading soles will be ready for use the following morning.

Should you need to replace a worn carpet sole while fishing, you can get by with waiting only about twenty minutes for the cement to dry (under such emergency circumstances). You must, of course, dry thoroughly the bottom of the shoe or boot before you apply the cement for replacing the sole. Spare soles and cement can be carried in one's wading vest or tackle box.

Since wading shoes are quite expensive, some anglers who are obliged to observe a fishing budget find that ordinary tennis shoes— the lace-above-the-ankles kind with plain rubber soles—work quite well, instead, even though the construction is of ligher material, and there are no watér escape holes (screened against sand entry, in the case of regular wading shoes).

Kite Fishing

One day, about fifteen years ago, a friend and fellow surf fishing enthusiast—Domina Jalbert—told me with a grin that he had perfected a new way to fish from an ocean beach.

"I can now cast out fifteen hundred feet," boasted the Boca Raton, Florida, aerologist and inventor.

Thereupon Dom showed me how he used a small cloth kite to carry his bait far offshore. Once in position, he could cause the bait to skip invitingly across the surface, by manipulating the kite. Or the bait could be allowed to sink to the bottom, instead.

This method of fishing has since become quite popular in Florida, from boats as well as from shore. Kite fishing is done from boats that are anchored, drifting or under way. In the last case the boat must move into the wind.

A typical kite outfit consists of a piece of husky fabric, cut perhaps thirty-six inches square. The cloth is kept stretched taut by crisscrossed plastic or aluminum rods. The ends of each rod fit into pockets at opposite corners of the kite fabric. The kite bridle is adjusted so the point of line pull is about at the center of the kite, where the braces (usually two) cross.

Several hundred yards of 40 to 60 pound test kite line is kept stored, and ready for use, on a large wooden reel. This reel is a simple affair; similar to an oversized 1:1 ratio fly reel. It is mounted on a short rod, the butt of which can be fit inside a conventional gunwale type fishing rod holder.

A release pin—usually of fiber, and similar to a clothespin—is attached to the kite line. This pin, in turn, grips a small metal guide (an eyelet) through which passes the fishing line.

The kite is flown by simultaneously releasing line from both the kite reel and the fishing reel on the angler's held rod. When the fishing line has been carried out the desired distance, the kite reel is locked to hold the kite at that position. The fishing line must then be reeled in—or let out, as required—to permit a small live fish, the usual bait, to skip and swim and splash invitingly at the surface.

(*Note:* had you merely clipped the kite's clothespin to your line— instead of using the eyelet—it would not be possible to reel in, or let out line, thus.)

When the strike comes, the force is such that it easily pulls the fishing line free of the kite—much as an ordinary trolled line is pulled free from the line-holding pin on an outrigger. The kite is then allowed to remain in the sky, while you fight the fish. The kite need be brought in only to rebait.

Commercial kite fishing kits can also be purchased, should you prefer not to make your own from scratch.

Fishing Through the Ice

Your fishing sport need not come to a halt when fall colors disappear and winter holds the rivers and lakes motionless in an icy grip. For then, despite the frosty air and often dark, snow-threatening skies, you can enjoy an excitingly different kind of sport: ice fishing.

Certain game fish continue to swim and forage for food beneath the ice, even during deepest winter. Included in this list are panfish like perch, crappie, bluegills and bullheads. Larger fish like muskellunge, northern and other pikes, trout, whitefish, walleye—even sturgeon—are also taken, both with natural and artificial baits.

You should wear warm clothing for protection against the bitter winds that can sweep across open ice. Today there is available for the ice fisherman a fine variety of lightweight and efficient outer and underclothing (the down-filled kind, in particular). Keeping one's feet warm usually poses the biggest problem. The insulated type boot has proven a blessing for many winter anglers who suffer from poor blood circulation in their feet. You should experiment with various kinds of footgear and socks. I know anglers who use the electrically heated type of socks.

Sunglasses should be worn for protection against ice and snow glare.

Ice fishing is mainly a fresh water sport, and the winter angler should frequent those sites where he would expect to find fish during the warm seasons. He should cut his hole in the ice only where he knows fish are present—or where he has good reason to believe they should be present (based upon the information provided earlier in this book). As has already been pointed out, for example, game fish will congregate at the mouth of a small waterway that empties into a lake, waiting for this feeder stream to carry natural food to them, just as it would were there no ice present.

For the sake of safety an ice angler should not fish alone. Nor should he *ever* take a chance by venturing out upon ice that is of doubtful strength (thickness). It is true that after a good freeze it is possible to drive an auto or snowmobile safely out upon river and lake ice, perhaps even towing an ice fishing shanty, mounted on runners, or a sled or toboggan loaded with firewood, chairs and other fishing gear. But do not take risks by yourself. Go where you see others. Sometimes—especially on weekends, when wives and children can be present—you may encounter entire "villages" of such ice fishermen's shanties. These can make quite an impressive sight, with their many glistening lights, after dark on a cold winter night.

The hole which the ice fisherman cuts is usually twelve to eighteen inches in diameter. An ax or chisel can be used. But an ice auger does a neater job. And the auger leaves fewer sharp edges to endanger your line.

The line can be lowered from a conventional rod and reel, although a special—shorter—rod is preferred, if a rod is used at all. It is much more convenient to use what is called a "tip-up" rig, instead. This method permits one to fish several holes at once. (Be sure to check local laws, to learn whether tip-ups are permitted, and how many.)

Tip-up rigs vary somewhat in design. One popular type involves two crossed sticks, each long enough to span the hole, with a reel attached to the end of a third stick that is also part of the assembly. When a fish strikes, the reel turns, allowing a stiff wire to spring upward, with a small warning flag at the end. This tells the angler that he's had a strike. The fish is then handlined to the surface. The hook is removed, and rebaited if necessary. The tip-up is reset and returned to its position over the hole.

After this, the angler probably returns to his stove-heated ice shanty, should he be fortunate enough to have one. Should he be operating quite a few tip-ups, some of them quite distant from his base of operations (usually, they are not) he may find it to his advantage to cover the distances involved on ice skates.

Live minnows are probably the ice fisherman's favorite bait. However, worms, grubs, pieces of fish or meat—even carrots and other vegetables, under certain conditions—are also used successfully. Some ice anglers prefer to use the more sporting artificial lure approach: jigs, spoons, spinners—even special weighted flies.

The minnow should be hooked in a manner so it will remain alive (refer to Chapter 3), then lowered to within a foot or two of the bottom. (Make a sounding, first, with a weighted line, to determine both the water depth and nature of the bottom.) This is usually a good position for walleyes and muskies. Perch, on the other hand, often feed right on the bottom. If strikes prove slow in coming, try chumming with small bits of bait dropped down through the hole.

If you are using artificials, these should be given greatly reduced movement, keeping in mind that in cold temperatures fish move much more slowly. Jig, spoon, spinner or whatever other lure, should be raised and lowered slowly, and imparted with whatever other movement the small hole opening permits. Don't expect the fish to hit as hard as they might at other times of the year. Nor will they pursue your offering with enthusiasm, should you pull it away too soon. The successful ice fisherman needs a special extra sense to tell him the precise time to set the hook, it sometimes appears.

You will also need a folding chair, or a box, to sit on. And a small dip net will spare you wet (and hence freezing!) fingers as you lift fresh bait from the minnow bucket. The little net will also help you keep the hole clear of small pieces of ice.

Observe others as you fish. Ask questions. After a few such trips you will learn how best to use a tip-up; how to make and use a canvas windbreak—even how to build your own ice shanty.

Proper Care for Tackle, Boat and Trailer

Tackle care involves more than merely washing off the rod and reel after use. Did you know, for example, that if you fail to release the drag tension on your reel—before you set it aside at day's end, following a tussle with a stubborn fish—that this oversight can permanently damage the reel's braking mechanism? Here's why: during the battle friction was developed at the surface of the drag components—heat was released in the process that in turn expanded the metal and plastic washers and possibly other material used in the reel's braking assembly. With the drag adjustment left on (screwed down tightly) it became impossible for these swollen components to contract to normal size later.

Result: rough spots may remain that now will cause the drag to act in an uneven, jerky manner when you next try to use it. Should the damage be severe, these sudden "grabs" at the line may well cause it to break during a following battle with an active fish. (To check whether your drag is uneven, adjust it for about half strength, then watch for continued spasmodic rod tip movement as an assistant pulls line at an even rate from the vertically held rod.)

The same uneven drag effect—this time on a slipping, rather than a grabbing, basis—can result from carelessly over-oiling a reel. In both cases you can sometimes "burn in" the drag, so that it becomes fairly even once more, by adjusting the reel for perhaps one third maximum drag resistance, then pulling off all the line from the spool—several times, if necessary, always at the same steady rate—to wear down the rough places, or burn off the oil. If this fails, the drag components will have to be replaced.

Another precaution to be observed: do not leave a spoolful of tightly stretched monofilament line on your reel, following a hard battle with a fish. Mono left under tension thus will develop great outward pressure—against the reel end plates—when it tries to return to its normal diameter, later. Reel spools have been hopelessly split thus, in the past, particularly before the introduction of the more expensive spools that are lathed from a single block of metal.

Modern reels are designed to be easily lubricated—even in the field, while fishing. But don't overdo it. Usually a drop of oil here and there, a small ribbon of gear grease, is all that is needed. Check the manufacturer's instruction sheet that came with the reel.

Don't use oil where grease is recommended, and vice versa. And use only lubricants specifically designed for reel use. Common household (sewing machine) oil, for example, can result in too much friction, nor does it work as well in the presence of water.

At least once a year you should completely overhaul each reel, or have someone else do so who is capable. If you do the job yourself, lay out each piece—on a cleared table or bench—in the order that it was removed. Then, when you reassemble the reel, you can restore the pieces in the reverse order. Have the manufacturer's instruction sheet—which usually provides a blown-apart sketch of the various parts, and how they fit together—handy for a reference. Do not try to force two surfaces together; everything is designed to fit easily, when the reassembly has been performed properly. And keep in mind that the non-rusting reel bolts are usually of softer than normal metal; don't risk breaking them off by using a screwdriver of improper size, or by applying too much pressure. A snug tightening is sufficient.

Your reel, even the simplest single-action fly reel, has more working parts than any other piece of your tackle. Hence it is apt to give the most trouble, if not properly maintained. A single piece of sand can sometimes jam the gear mechanism in a way that will cause harmful wear. So flush out the reel with carbon tetrachloride, or some other suitable solvent, without delay, should dirt enter the reel housing. After this, wipe the parts dry with a soft cloth and relubricate.

I have friends, big game saltwater anglers, who refuse to wash off their tackle with fresh water, in the usually recommended manner, after a day of sport. Instead, they wipe off the rod and reel, then spray the metal parts with one of the penetrating lubricants (such as WD-40). This, the anglers claim, prevents the force of the water rinse from carrying salt crystals deeper into the reel mechanism.

In any event, tackle that has not been specifically designed for saltwater use (i.e., which does not have stainless steel hardware) should be given preventive maintenance immediately after each use. In fact, it is a good idea to apply a light coating of oil to the reel's exterior surfaces, to the rod guides and reel seat, before each use.

Rods should be carried, and shipped, when necessary, inside suitable strong fiber or metal cases. Many a fishing trip has been ruined because some careless person slammed a car door, or trunk lid, upon a favorite stick. Or perhaps because the rod was placed carelessly in the bottom of a boat (gunwale hangers should be provided), or leaned haphazardly against a rock or tree (place it inside a bush, with the tip clear), and a fishing companion—even a guide—stepped upon it.

Should a glass rod be broken thus in the field it is sometimes possible to make on-the-spot repairs that will permit you to continue fishing. In fact, repairs so made often prove so satisfactory that the angler is quite content to continue using the fiber glass rod as is. This is particularly true should the break occur close to the tip, or near a ferrule.

To make such a repair, first cut off square the end of each broken piece. Then select a plug—usually not over three inches long, the length being dependent upon the rod diameter involved. The plug should be of a diameter that will allow it to slide easily inside each broken piece. (Nearly all glass rods are hollow.) Ideally, this plug will be a piece of lightweight spring steel, since this material should not noticeably affect the rod's whippy action. Satisfactory plugs have been made, too, however, from a small piece of hollow tubing, or a wooden dowel of suitable diameter, even a nail or heavy piece of wire.

Next, apply a good grade of epoxy cement inside one of the broken ends. Do the same to one half of the plug that is to be used. Then slide this cemented half of the plug snugly inside the broken end. Next repeat this procedure with the second broken rod piece, cementing it and the remaining half of the plug.

Bring the two ends of the plug-reinforced rod firmly together, making sure that the rod guides are in alignment as you do so. Fill in the crack at the joint, if necessary, with a small additional amount of cement. Then wipe this joint neatly clean. Set the rod aside for the epoxy to harden (usually twenty-four hours are required).

A split bamboo rod is something else. I have made temporary (i.e., external splint type) repairs in the field. But I believe most anglers will agree it is best to send such a rod to the maker, or a skilled craftsman, for proper repair (perhaps replacement of the entire damaged section).

When hard wear indicates the need, the guide windings of both glass and cane rods can be touched up, using a good grade of varnish. Sometimes it is advantageous to revarnish a cane rod completely.

Grooved, nicked or otherwise damaged rod guides can cause excessive line wear, and should be replaced. Remove the offending guide be carefully cutting free its holding threads, using a razor blade or sharp knife to do this. Place the new guide, of identical size and design, in the same spot, being careful to line it up with the other guides on the rod. (To make sure of this, temporarily tape one foot of the guide in position against the rod.) Exact replacement guides, tips, ferrules—even reel seats—can usually be purchased from the manufacturer, as can winding thread of original size and color—should you make your own rod repairs.

After the replacement guide has been wound securely into position, apply a coating of epoxy cement, or several coats of rod varnish, and set the repair aside to dry overnight.

A lost or damaged tip can be replaced with a new one in similar manner. If the angler is lucky, and it is necessary to reposition the tip but a few inches below its original position, it is doubtful much difference in rod action will be noticed.

Often ferrules become dirty and stuck—especially when saltwater corrosion has been allowed to take place. When this happens do not yield to the temptation to twist loose the frozen joint. Instead, a mild application of heat—often the flame from a wooden match will prove sufficient—will usually solve the problem. If not, apply some penetrating type oil, and give it time to soak in. Then, squat down, holding the stuck portion of the rod inside your bent knees. Your hands, meanwhile, should grip the rod firmly, one hand positioned just outside each knee. Now force the knees slowly, but steadily, outward. Nearly always, the pressure so developed will break loose the stubborn joint.

Once the stuck ferrules have been parted, proceed to clean away the corrosion with a solvent (even gasoline will often do), then smooth the metal with a strip of crocus cloth, or perhaps very fine sandpaper. Work this in a moving-belt type manner about all surfaces of the male ferrule, and wrap a piece of the abrasive cloth or paper about a small, circular probe for the female portion.

Never apply oil to ferrules, in the mistaken belief that this lubrication will insure that they will come apart easily, later. Instead, the oil creates what amounts to an airtight lock. To lubricate a ferrule properly, run the male portion through the hair a few times, or place it against one side of your nose, and turn it a few times.

A broken rod handle, or one with worn reel seat threads, can likewise be replaced and reglued—using a replacement handle gotten from the manufacturer, or perhaps some well-stocked tackle store. Unless you are handy with tools, however, this job would be best done by the manufacturer, or a qualified repairman.

The cork areas of rod handles can become quite dirty. They can be cleaned with soap powder, then smoothed off with fine sandpaper.

Metal lures, particularly spoons and spinners, have a tendency to discolor and corrode, especially when used in salt water. They can be cleaned with a fine grade of steel wool (silver polish should be used for chromed and stainless steel surfaces), then given a light coat of clear lacquer. Wooden plugs that have been bitten and scarred from contact with rocks, etc., can have their gouges and holes filled with plastic wood, then repainted with the original colors. The effort is worthwhile, when one considers that such lures may cost from a dollar to two-fifty or more to replace.

The hooks seem to rust and deteriorate first on such lures. For this reason I use a small brush and paint the hooks—and other metal surfaces while I am at it—with a light coating of melted reel grease between fishing trips.

Modern fishing lines require little care. Just keep them dry—if they are used infrequently—and, in the case of fly lines, reasonably clean.

Flies should not be stored away while moist. Dry them in the sun, or near some source of heat. The hair or feather dressings can be rejuvenated by "fluffing" them in a steam stream emanating from a boiling teakettle. Dressings should be checked for tightness, and rewound if necessary. A drop of fly dope will often secure a loose dressing, and give prolonged life. Dry flies and surface bugs should be carefully dipped in—or sprayed with—silicone waterproofing material. And some moth flakes will protect stored flies.

The angler's rain gear, waders, wading shoes, boots, fishing vest or jacket, may also be considered tackle items and should likewise be given suitable care. Holes should be patched in boots and waders, torn garments sewn and rebuttoned, etc. Do not store away boots and garments that are moist, for this invites mildew and rot. I've observed friends dry their boots and waders near furnaces, even with light bulbs. But the safest way I've found is to stuff the feet with newspaper. This absorbs the moisture. You may have to change the paper inside the boots or waders several times. Then hang them, feet uppermost, in a cool, dry place.

The only safe use I've found for a light bulb around a pair of waders, or boots, is to place such light source temporarily inside—in a darkened room—to indicate what holes may be present, to cause the wader or boot to leak.

Fishing vests and jackets—vests, especially—have a tendency to accumulate all sorts of moisture-holding paraphernalia. The pockets should be cleaned and dried out at regular intervals—especially the larger pocket that may be used to carry home fish.

Willow creels aren't nearly as popular as they once were. But, if used, they should be washed thoroughly at reasonable intervals with a detergent or soda solution. Varnish the creel both inside and out, too, when this appears necessary.

The care you give your boat will depend to some extent upon its size. It is much easier, for example, to inspect and treat a damaged hull if it rests on a trailer, than it would be if the boat must first be pulled from the water. Nevertheless, the care and treatments are quite similar.

Physical damage to hull or superstructure is, of course, a main source of difficulty. Learn how to dock or beach your boat properly despite the influence of wind or tide. (Refer to Chapter 8.) Paint can be scraped from a wooden hull, for example, the result of carelessly striking a dock. Moisture can penetrate, and the hull can rot. Again, a fiber glass hull that suffers such injury, or which perhaps becomes abrased from careless contact with gravel beach or rocks, may have its glass fibers exposed, so that blisters form.

Corrosion is perhaps the next most common difficulty. Metal hulls used in salt or brackish water should be hosed down after each use, and metal fixtures wiped clean. Such hardware should be of corrosion resistant alloy for saltwater use. And possible electrolysis damage between metals should be avoided by keeping such metals separate, even if both be of the corrosion resistant variety. (If the metals must come in contact, first paint them with a primer of zinc chromate.) Do not risk similar adverse reactions by using anti-fouling paint on an aluminum hull.

The inside of any boat should be kept dry, not an easy task. Bilges should be kept drained. Sponge up any remaining water. A free circulation of cabin air will help. Those small boatmen who cover their craft tightly with a tarp or tailored canvas cover are inviting moisture from condensation—inside—when the temperature changes outside, as it will. Allow for frequent airing out. At reasonable intervals dry out life jackets, cushions, bunk mattresses, etc., by carrying these out into the sun. Moisture can be the boatman's great enemy: rusting tackle, tools, engine, etc., etc.

Like a car, or other piece of movable equipment, a boat will last only as long—and perform satisfactorily—as your treatment of it allows. The speed jockey who persists in allowing his boat hull to pound excessively against rough water will soon find things working loose. Don't be a neglectful skipper.

Your boat trailer, also, will readily suffer from corrosion if it is used for saltwater launchings and not washed off thoroughly with fresh water after each use. A common mistake made by those launching in salt water is to back the trailer so far down the ramp that the wheels become completely submerged. This should not be necessary, provided the usual tilt-frame type trailer is used. And it simply invites seepage of salt water past the wheel bearing hub seals, and into the axle. Once that happens you can be on the road to serious difficulty. The wise boatmen backs his rig into the water until only the tires are submerged. (Incidentally, the condition of the wheel bearing grease should be checked every 1,000 miles.)

Paint that shows signs of blistering and rusting on the trailer frame should be scraped away, and the metal underneath sanded clean before the spot is repainted. If the trailer's rubber rollers show signs of deep grouging, or other serious wear, replace them. (This is easy to do; exact replacements can be purchased from the manufacturer.) Replace the carpet stripping (which is usually nylon) on the movable hull-cradling boards when these become frayed and worn.

At fairly frequent intervals check that all trailer bolts are secure. Lubricate the winch gearing and coupling mechanism as may prove necessary. If the winch line, be it a rope or small metal cable, shows signs of rot or fraying, replace it without delay. Check that whatever means is used to hold the boat in position atop the trailer—usually it is a length of nylon webbing, with take-up buckle—is capable of doing this securely. Boat supply stores sell such hold-down devices, should a replacement be needed.

Use a good grade of heavy grease (such as Lubriplate No. 70) to lubricate the guide roller bearings periodically, the tilt-frame and cradle mechanisms. Machine oil, about 30 weight, should be used on the coupler mechanism that fits over the ball hitch. The hitch itself should have a light coating of grease smeared over it. The ball should also be kept clean, and free of rust.

You can pack your own wheel bearings, as I do, but if you doubt your ability to do this, a garage or service station will. It is a good idea, while on a trip, to check the temperature of the wheel hubs at each gas stop. The hub should not feel hot to the touch, since this indicates trouble: probably the lack of suitable lubrication.

Do not overload your trailer—a common fault. It was designed to support the weight of the boat and motor—not the additional weight of a tent, ice chests, and other items that customarily are loaded aboard. If in doubt, have the trailer weighed, then deduct this weight from the total of trailer and boat. The trailer manufacturer will tell you how much weight it can safely transport.

Too, keep in mind that boat trailer tires operate at a higher pressure than your auto tires, as a rule. Here is a guide, subject to confirmation by the maker of the particular brand of tires you may be using: 65 pounds of pressure for 400×8, 400×12, and 530×12 tires; 60 pounds for 6×9 tires; 50 pounds for 575-500×8 tires.

How Safely to Trailer a Boat

I have already mentioned overloading and improper tire pressure, two common causes of unsafe trailer operation. Another source of difficulty, and probably the most dangerous of all, is the driver's inability to drive and maneuver safely while the trailer is in tow. This seems to be particularly true when backing up is involved.

This driving problem can be corrected by practice. Select a large, vacant area to practice parking the trailer. (A school parking lot on a weekend, for example.) Set up several empty cardboard boxes, or other markers, and practice with these as targets while you try to back in a straight line, or stop at a proper imaginary point to "launch," or to park parallel to a non-existent curb. A good side-view mirror will help greatly—the truck type that projects outward to give a clear view rearward.

Before moving your craft on a trailer you must make sure that each fits the other. The trailer's rubber rollers should provide adequate keel support from the transom forward, to the start of the bow. The fore and aft cradles (there should be at least two on each side) should be adjustable and capable of holding the hull snugly and erect. The hold-down strap should prevent vertical movement.

A trailer that is properly balanced to its load will present at least fifty pounds of measurable weight where its tongue attaches to the ball hitch on the towing car. (It may be even more—for this proper weight represents, generally, about 5 per cent of the total weight of boat, motor and equipment. If you are towing a rig of 1,500 pounds gross weight, therefore, the tongue weight should be around seventy-five pounds.) Proper towing balance is achieved when the trailer neither sways excessively (an indication that the rig is tail-heavy) nor pushes against the car, when you slow down, to a degree where it affects the steering while traveling on a fairly even road.

To meet state licensing requirements your trailer will have to be equipped with adequate stop, turn and license tag lights. Check the connecting cable often for proper operation, for wear. (Water tends to corrode the connectors; a dragging cable soon wears through.) Red reflective tape, affixed to the transom of the boat, can prove an added safety factor, should the lights fail.

Your car brakes should be kept in good condition, to handle the trailer's added weight. If the towed rig is a large one, state law likely will require that the trailer have its own brakes. The "surge" type of hydraulic trailer brake has become popular. This brake operates automatically when the towing car slows down, then releases as you speed up. However, electrically operated trailer brakes are also used.

For greatest safety the trailer towing hitch should be mounted directly on the car's frame—not merely clamped to the rear bumper. And there should be at least one safety chain that can be used to join car and trailer, for added security. Some states require two chains.

I have found it advisable to carry a spare wheel with inflated tire. You can spend half a day trying to find a replacement tire—much less replace a damaged wheel—in the remote areas that fishermen frequent! And your car bumper jack, by the way, will nearly always prove useless in changing a trailer wheel. Carry, instead, a scissors or similar small jack that will fit under the low trailer axle.

Finally, practice taking corners; learn the need for swinging wider than usual when making a right- or left-hand turn. For a trailer invariably turns in a shorter space—and you will find yourself running over the curbing, or someone's lawn, if you don't swing purposely wide. Learn the need for "laying back" on a highway until you are *sure* it is safe to overtake and pass another vehicle. For now you will not have the pickup ordinarily provided by your car, the pickup you are used to. And do not cut back into the original driving lane until you are certain you have allowed for ample clearance for your trailer. Use turn signals for both operations. Give yourself more time—and distance—also, when slowing and stopping. For now, of course, you have considerably more weight that must be braked.

How to Prevent Theft of Boat and Tackle

Only a few years ago it was considered a novelty to have your outboard motor stolen from your boat after dark by a scuba diving thief. No more. In this permissive era of drugs and other expensive habits, burglary has become our fastest growing crime. A bold new breed of crook—friendly and as innocent-appearing as a Scoutmaster —has found it most profitable to prey upon this country's hordes of sportsmen. And he does this by specializing in daylight robbery.

Favorite victims are campers who foolishly feel safe because they are surrounded by others in the outdoors; boaters who leave their craft at day's end in some large marina with a false sense of security; anglers who mistakenly believe that their expensive tackle is safe simply because it is locked inside the car—or even in a closet at home.

Today's thief can afford to be brazen. He knows that, even if caught, he will escape with but a light larceny or misdemeanor fine. For he strikes while you are absent, hence has no use for a gun; no need to inflict bodily harm. Instead, he studies your daily habits as he camps or fishes nearby, waiting to make off with your boat or other equipment while you are absent, purchasing supplies, or whatever.

Often this crook and his companions will pose as members of a service organization—complete with uniforms and truck—perhaps playing the role of boat repairmen, propane gas suppliers, etc. And there seems to be no limit to their boldness. One of New York City's largest sporting goods stores was recently victimized thus, in a daring daylight robbery. Several neatly uniformed "employees" of a well-known outboard manufacturing concern arrived at the store's shipping platform with a phony merchandise pickup order. They then proceeded nonchalantly to load into their truck, likewise marked with deceiving insignia, some $5,000 worth of motors. Not until these brazen thieves had driven off with their loot was the error discovered. One of the unsuspecting employees who had helped load the motors was a store security guard!

There is little that an honest citizen can do, unfortunately, to prevent thieves from breaking and entering into his car or home. More than 1,500,000 such "B and E" cases take place each year—so many that police morale has slumped considerably (there simply aren't enough cops to go around). And more than half of these burglaries are within the home. My own home was robbed twice within thirteen months. I lost my choicest fishing tackle, guns, cameras, etc. And, although the serial numbers of nearly every item were provided the authorities, nothing was ever recovered.

In fact, the extent of the police "investigation" amounted to little more than taking a record of what was stolen. When, from sheer frustration, I began to investigate on my own, and produced latent fingerprints on several pieces of broken window glass, the officers still evidenced but small interest. Only my long-time insurance company took positive action. They promptly canceled my home owner's policy —this in spite of the fact such companies are chartered to do business on the basis of such calculated risks.

About the only thing the honest citizen has working in his behalf, where a robbery is being committed, is the time element. The daytime thief is obliged to move quickly. He will invariably pass up one object in favor of another, should the first be the most difficult of the two to make off with quickly. For this reason, it is to your advantage—while away from camp or dock—to loop a long length of lightweight chain about a tree trunk, a piling (below the dock's deck)—perhaps through a car or trailer wheel, instead, should one be handy—then through the handles of portable boat gasoline tanks, folding camp table, suitcases, etc., before joining the chain ends with a sturdy padlock.

Some trailer boatmen carrry an eight-inch concrete building block with them. They use this to support the trailer after one wheel has been removed to thwart theft. Admitted, the extra time required to do this can prove annoying—but well worthwhile, too.

The boatman who is obliged to leave his craft unattended in some slip, or in his backyard, or an apartment parking space, should first remove from sight all tempting loose objects like fire extinguisher, anchor, chairs, cushions, fishing tackle, etc. In addition, should the nature of the transom on an outboard hull be such that you can loop and lock a chain between it and the removable motor (or even between a thwart seat and the engine), do so. But keep in mind that even the sturdiest chain can easily be cut in your absence.

As for the home, or apartment, where you live: do *not* store rods in one corner of the closet in the master bedroom. By their own admission, that is the first place thieves look for the owner's most prized sporting equipment. Instead, walk about your quarters. Ask yourself where would be the least likely place a fast-moving crook would be inclined to search for a choice fly rod, etc. Then place your prized equipment there, even if it should be less convenient than usual to do this.

Electronic Fish Locators

These scientific devices for finding fish have recently become quite popular, although the first such depth finder was developed nearly twenty years ago. This writer has never used one, preferring to try and outwit his fish in the usual, more sporting way—particularly since fish populations are dwindling discouragingly these days. Nevertheless, fishermen do go fishing to catch fish. Angling has become a rather expensive hobby, and it is understandable that some anglers should attach more importance to meat than method.

Basically, the electronic fish locator functions in this manner: a series of ultrasonic (inaudible) sound waves are projected bottomward—in the shape of an inverted ice cream cone—by that part of the sonar equipment known as the "transducer." This unit is in physical contact with the water, and, soon as the descending sound waves strike any object between the surface and the bottom that is of a density different from the water—be it a submerged tree, a rocky ledge, a fish or whatever—the sound waves are bounced back to be recorded as "blips" of light on the calibrated scope of a receiver unit that is also a part of the fish locator. Since the speed of a sound wave in water is a constant (the wave travels four times faster than it would in the air), the distance to the interfering object so struck can be automatically computed, based upon the time required for the echo so to rebound.

With some practice, the user of the locator can interpret the light signals to tell the depth of water under his hull, the contour of the bottom, whether it is rocky or muddy, etc.

There are two general types of these locators: the portable and the gimbal-mounted variety. Both operate on the principle already described. The former is about the size of a small tackle box and has its own built-in power supply. It is used mostly by small boaters. In operation, the receiver portion of the portable unit is placed in some convenient place inside the boat, while the transducer is fastened to the side or transom, by means of a suction cup or a clamp-on type bracket. Since water turbulence (air bubbles) will result in false readings, the boat speed must not exceed about six miles per hour. Nor can accurate readings be made while crossing wakes, or while backing up.

The more complex, or so-called gimbal-type, locator is built in and will give readings at speeds of better than thirty mph, provided its transducer is mounted where it will not be in turbulent water (usually through the hull, near the stern). Gimbal-mounted fish locators are usually powered from the boat's battery.

Both portable and gimbal fish finders show on their dials either a blip or a band of light to indicate both the zero mark and the echo mark (light) that indicates depth.

How to Clean and Cook Fish Properly

Where cleaning their catch is involved, there seem to be two general classes of anglers. The first do the job with a sharp knife and a few deft slices. The others clumsily leave inside the fish annoying bones, waste too much of the flesh and generally produce torn, uneven fillets that often seem to resemble mutilated pieces of cardboard ripped from some hapless carton.

After some thirty years of fish cleaning, this is one of the simplest ways I've found to do the job: Place the whole fish on a table or other flat surface, unscaled and ungutted. With a suitably long, thin-bladed knife make a single downward cut, just behind the gill cover, to the backbone. Next, cut deeply along the backbone—right down to the rib cage—nearly to the tail. Then use short, slicing strokes to trim away all possible flesh from the rib cage (which extends about two thirds the length of the fish). Sliced thus, from backbone to belly, this will leave you with a neat fillet that ends at the tail.

Turn the fish over and repeat the operation. Discard the head, the now practically meatless backbone, and the entrails.

Finally, neatly separate each fillet from its skin (and hence automatically from any scales, too). This is done by placing the fillet, skin side down, on a flat surface. Apply steady finger pressure (or that from a fork) to the very end of the tail. Make a small starting cut there, then slide the blade between skin and meat, working toward the wide end of the fillet once more with short, slicing strokes. Result: a neat, boneless fillet.

This easy, foolproof method for filleting fish can be used for anything from catfish to dolphin. Some fish, like trout, do not require scaling, so you can leave the skin intact, if you prefer.

A variation of the above method that is preferred by some anglers is first to make deep cuts, one on each side, close alongside the dorsal and belly fins, then lift out these fins and their associated bones before beginning the filleting operation. (If you simply use the knife, or a pair of heavy scissors, to cut off these fins, as many fishermen do, you leave the annoying small bones in the fish, to make eating difficult later.)

Cooking methods will vary considerably with individual taste. Most any cookbook will give details how to broil, fry and bake fish; how to prepare fish chowders, sauces and so on. Generally, the sooner a fish is eaten, the better will be the taste. My mouth waters at memories of broiled bluefish eaten within the hour after being taken from some wave-pounded ocean beach; or trout that were pan-fried right on the stream bank. If there must be a delay between the catching and the eating, as there often is, at least make sure that the fish is properly cleaned and iced down within a reasonable time. Fish that are allowed to dry out in the sun, often to become entrail-soured, make poor meals.

One delicious method for preparing fish, often overlooked by the average angler, is smoking. Many fishermen foolishly consider this something to be attempted only by the gourmet type cook. Actually, it is simple, inexpensive and serves as a fine way (especially for campers) to preserve part of the catch for later use.

Probably the simplest way to smoke your own fish is to purchase one of the small, electrically heated smokers on the market. However, if you prefer, you can make your own unit from an old oil drum, etc.

The commercial smoker is a simple metal box, with a lid, that measures about twenty inches on all sides. It has a removable, multi-shelved wire grill upon which is laid the fish to be smoked. And, at the bottom of the box, there is an electric hotplate.

The gutted and washed fish are first soaked for twenty-four to forty-eight hours, depending upon size (an average-size fish can be smoked whole; a large one may have to be filleted, or cut into steaks), in a brine solution consisting of three quarters of a cup of salt per gallon of water. Be sure that all bloody flesh is first removed, including the dark backbone strip that is the fish's kidney. The fish are then placed in position. Next, a small (fry-type) metal pan is filled with either wood chips or sawdust, and placed atop the hotplate. This will produce the smoke needed to cure the meat.

Hickory wood is used most often. Some smokery enthusiasts prefer cherry, green apple and other kinds, however.

Adjust the hotplate so a small, but steady, volume of smoke is produced. Too much smoke, too soon, can leave a bitter taste in the prematurely cured meat. If the chips or sawdust char too quickly, sprinkle them lightly with water. Six to twelve hours is the usual curing time, depending upon how rich a flavor is desired. About once each hour brush a light coating of cooking oil over the fish, inside and out.

Properly smoked fish will have a golden brown color, and can be eaten immediately.

Sportsmanship and Conservation

In concluding this book it would hardly seem necessary to emphasize the need for preserving the wonderful natural resources with which God has blessed our country. Yet there are those who continue to squander foolishly, to litter and pollute, to grab selfishly at the expense of those who must come after. If there is still time to provide a solution for this, the answer must involve education. Those of us who have already experienced the best that the great outdoors had to offer must now take time to train our young people patiently—so that they, in turn, can educate their children—how best to enjoy what has been left.

We must set the example by returning to the water, unharmed, that extra fish (if not all of them!) that we know deep inside we really do not need, regardless *how* big it may be. We must pick up the litter of others, and plead anew the need for keeping the waters clean, for making sure campfires are out, and all the rest.

For, only if we are firmly resolved to make this effort, I believe, will those who come hopefully wading and boating after us be able to echo what Captain John Smith wrote more than 350 years ago: "What sport doth yield a more pleasing content, and less hurt or charge, than angling with a hook."

GEORGE X. SAND has written hundreds of articles on fishing for *Field & Steam, Outdoor Life* and *Sports Afield* and has become well known among fishing enthusiasts. He has also written *Skin and Scuba Diving, Salt Water Fly Fishing, The Everglades Today, Endangered Wilderness* and a book of juvenile fiction, *Iron Tail*. Mr. Sand lives in Florida and fishes often.

Index